IN THE NAME OF SALVATION

Three Theological Treatises

IN THE NAME OF SALVATION

Three Theological Treatises

~ + ~

JAMES THOMAS ANGELIDIS

In the Name of Salvation:
Three Theological Treatises

James Thomas Angelidis

www.jtangelidis.com

First published by James Thomas Angelidis 2016.
This second edition published (as it appears in
Approaching the Kingdom: An Anthology)
by James Thomas Angelidis 2017.

Reprinted with no revisions to literature (second edition). Included with this reprint, at the end, is the article "In the Spirit of Truth: Identifying My Three Theological Treatises in Church Tradition."
Also included is a works cited list.
Reprinted 2024.

Cover Design:
Layout by James Thomas Angelidis.

Author Image:
(On author bio page) Photograph taken of self by
James Thomas Angelidis.

"every scribe who has been trained for the kingdom of heaven is like a householder who brings out of his treasure what is new and what is old."

- Jesus Christ (Matthew 13:52, RSV)

AUTHOR BIO

James Thomas Angelidis has been awarded three university degrees and has authored and independently published several Christian books. These accomplishments helped him become a Professor of Christian Theology at Seton Hall University in South Orange, New Jersey. Discover James's works on his website at www.jtangelidis.com.

ABOUT

I believe there is truth in the proverb, "The pen is mightier than the sword."

The damage done by the emperor's sword can be rectified by the writer's pen. Nothing can replace a life lost by the sword, but with the help of the pen, the story of that life can teach, inspire and unveil truth that can save many lives. When the emperor dies, so does his sword, as does his power and his influence on the world; yet, the writer's pen can leave a lasting impression unto the ages. The ideas behind the pen can change the world; something, the emperor tries to do with his sword, but inevitably fails. Certainly, if we dig deeper, we can discover additional meanings within the proverb's words, but it is clear that the pen is powerful. The pen can make a difference in people's lives and with the help of God, I hope to make a difference in people's lives with my pen. I hope to give life.

- James Thomas Angelidis

CONTENTS

TREATISE ONE

THE SUPREME TRANSFORMATION –
WATER INTO WINE

JAMES THOMAS ANGELIDIS

Introduction

The Bible is the most translated book in the world. It is widely accepted that the second most translated book in the world is the Tao Te Ching. Both books teach truths to the ready reader and if they are examined together, we can find evidence of Christ's impact on the world as the Son of God. He transformed the world as only the Son of God could have. Beyond the most profound influence of any man, He transformed the natural rhythm of the cosmos. This celestial transformation was foreshadowed by His first sign of transforming water into wine. In this treatise, through the Tao Te Ching and relevant sections of the Bible, we will examine our Lord's first sign of transforming water into wine and the truth it exposes about His impact on the cosmos. I believe if we can better understand the Tao as taught in the Tao Te Ching, we will be able to better see the magnitude, magnificence and majesty of Christ. In writing this treatise, I hope to help my fellow Christians better understand our Lord through knowledge of the Tao and to help non-Christians, through the Spirit of Truth, begin to believe that Christ is the Son of the Most High God.

The Tao Te Ching

The Tao Te Ching is the principal text of Taoism - an ancient Chinese philosophy that became one of the world's great religions. Probably a compilation of wisdom and insight from many sages, the Tao Te Ching began to take shape as far back as the seventh century before Christ, but most likely did not reach its final form until the mid-third century before Christ. However, tradition ascribes the authorship of the text to Lao Tzu, a seemingly legendary figure who is said to have been a contemporary of Confucius during the early sixth century before our Lord.

With 81 short poem-like chapters, the text is primarily concerned with the Tao and Te. Taoism adopted its name from the Tao, which translates into English as "Way," as in the way the cosmos operates. It is the primal life force that sustains the harmony and natural rhythm of the universe. It is the ineffable reality of the universe. From before the beginning of time, it is the mysterious source of Heaven and earth and the fountain of life for all life in the universe. Te translates into English as "Virtue," as in the virtue characteristic of one who abides by the Tao. It is the manifestation or power of the Tao in one who acts in accordance with the Tao. Ching means "classic work," so the Tao Te Ching neatly, yet roughly translates into "The Classic Work of the Way and its Virtue."

It is important to note that as I explicate the Tao Te Ching, there is no single definitive English translation of the text. There are, actually, over 100 translations of the text in English. Ancient Chinese does not translate easily into English, so there can be variation in translation. Jonathan Star explains that, "The nature of ancient Chinese is one reason why this scripture, for thousand of years, has 'baffled all inquiry.' Ancient Chinese is a conceptual language; it is unlike English and other Western languages, which are perceptual. Western languages are rooted in grammar that frames events in real time, identifies subject and object, clarifies relationships, and establishes temporal sequences. Ancient Chinese is based on pictorial representations, without grammar. Characters symbolize concepts that can be interpreted as singular or plural; as a noun, a verb, or an adjective; as happening in the past, present, or future. Therefore, when translating from Chinese to English, the Chinese characters must be framed within a perceptual context to be understood" (Jonathan Star, Tao Te Ching, 3 [see pages 3-7 for examples]). There are many who have made great efforts to bring the Tao Te Ching from the East to the West. Each translator interprets the text with his or her own understanding of the text to try to bring out the true meaning of the text. In English, I have discovered three solid translations that I believe do the text justice: the Stephen Addiss and Stanley Lombardo translation, the Gia-Fu Feng and Jane English translation, and the John C.H. Wu translation. These translations differ, but their essences are the same. I have used my discernment to use the three translations together and write about the Tao in the light of Christ to enlighten people about Christ.

The Tao and Water

The Tao is unfamiliar to many people, so I have explicated it below to the best of my abilities. It is important to understand what the Tao is and how it functions in order to appreciate and comprehend the magnitude of Christ, to understand who our Lord is and what He did as the Son of God.

In the Tao Te Ching, Chapter 21 provides an insightful description of the Tao:

> Now what is the Tao?
> It is Something elusive and evasive.
> Evasive and elusive!
> And yet it contains within Itself a Form.
> Elusive and evasive!
> And yet it contains within itself a substance
> Shadowy and dim!
> And yet It contains within Itself a Core of Vitality.
> The Core of Vitality is very real,
> It contains within Itself an unfailing Sincerity.
> Throughout the ages Its Name has been preserved
> In order to recall the Beginning of all things.

How do I know the ways of all things at the
Beginning?
By what is within me (Wu).

For peoples in the West, the teachings in the
Tao Te Ching are enigmatic and difficult to
comprehend. Though I was born and raised in the
West and have never visited the East, I have devoted
myself to the great world religions' sacred scriptures
and through studying them and my experiences as a
man in the world, I feel confident that I have a firm
grasp of the lessons to be learned in the Tao Te
Ching. Nonetheless, the first two lines of the text
illustrate the difficulty in conveying the meaning of
and discussing the Tao:

> Tao can be talked about, but not the Eternal
> Tao
> Names can be named, but not
> the Eternal Name (Wu, 1).

The nature of the Tao is described throughout
the text, but I believe Chapter 25 provides the most
comprehensive and acute description:

> Something unformed and
> complete
> Before heaven and earth were
> born,
> Solitary and silent,

Stands alone and unchanging,
Pervading all things without
limit.
It is like the mother of all under
heaven,
But I don't know its name -
Better call it Tao.
Better call it great.
Great means passing on.
Passing on means going far.
Going far means returning.
Therefore,
Tao is great,
And heaven,
And earth,
And humans,
Four great things in the world.
Aren't humans one of them?
Humans follow earth
Earth follows heaven
Heaven follows Tao.
Tao follows its own nature
(Addiss).

Trying to understand the Tao can be difficult -
whether one is from the East or the West, the North or
the South - and I believe few attempt to do so. In
Chapter 41, the Tao Te Ching teaches,

When a wise scholar hears the Tao,

He practices it diligently.
When a mediocre scholar hears the Tao,
He wavers between belief and unbelief.
When a worthless scholar hears the Tao,
He laughs boisterously at it.
But if such a one does not laugh at it,
The Tao would not be the Tao (Wu).

Upon reading this passage, I ask myself, "How many of us are wise scholars? How many of us have read about the Tao? How many of us are able to recognize the Tao?" And, I tell myself, "Few." Though I am certain there are great men and women who have not formally studied the Tao, who are unread, yet who are close to the Tao, I believe most people waver between belief and unbelief and many laugh. I believe few people devote themselves to the Tao and try to understand and live in union with it. In writing this treatise, I hope to awaken people to the Tao, to feed their hunger for something more in life and for God.

Water is a clear Taoist symbol and is used in the Tao Te Ching as a metaphor for the Tao. The Tao is ineffable and difficult to comprehend, yet water is compared with it to make it accessible to the human mind. There are a handful of metaphors in the Tao Te Ching that are used to pin down the elusive nature of the Tao, but water is chief among them as it is used to indicate the highest good. Chapter 8 is the principal chapter that elaborates on the metaphor of water.

In Chapter 8, we learn,

> The highest form of goodness is like water (Wu).

Tao is the highest good. More virtuous than virtue, Tao permeates the world and is made manifest in the form of Te in people who follow the Tao. It is beyond all other forms of goodness and is of the highest value. In chapter 38, we learn,

> Failing Tao, man resorts to Virtue.
> Failing Virtue, man resorts to humanity.
> Failing humanity, man resorts to morality.
> Failing morality, man resorts to ceremony.
> [And] ceremony is the merest husk of faith and loyalty (Wu).

Chapter 16 also illustrates the superior value of the Tao:

> Mind opening leads to compassion,
> Compassion leads to nobility,
> Nobility to heavenliness,
> Heavenliness to Tao (Addiss).

The highest good is the power of the Tao in the world and in people. The Tao behaves like water and I believe if we keep the image of flowing water in our minds, we can see the metaphor's truth in Chapter 73:

Heaven's Tao does not contend
But prevails,
Does not speak
But responds,
Is not summoned
But arrives,
Is utterly still
But plans all actions (Addiss).

The Waters in the Jewish Scriptures

In the beginning when the Uncreated God Created, His Spirit moved "over the face of the waters" (Genesis 1:2). The ancient Taoists were aware that there was Something "unformed and complete before heaven and earth were born" that behaved like water and assigned it the name Tao (Addiss, 25).

On the second day of Creation, God said, "Let there be a firmament in the midst of the waters, and let it separate the waters from the waters" (Genesis 1:6). God called the firmament Heaven with waters above and below. As mentioned, the ancient Taoists understood that there is Something above Heaven that behaves like water. The Jews, as well, were aware of the waters above the heavens. As the Psalmist exclaims,

Praise the Lord!

Praise the Lord from the heavens,
praise him in the heights!
2 Praise him, all his angels,
praise him, all his host!
3 Praise him, sun and moon,
praise him, all you shining stars!
4 Praise him, you highest heavens,
and you waters above the heavens!
5 Let them praise the name of the Lord!
For he commanded and they were created.
6 And he established them for ever and ever;
he fixed their bounds which cannot be
passed (Psalm 148:1, RSV).

The ancient Taoists did not know God, but both Taoists and Jews were aware of the waters above the heavens.

Te and Water

Like the Tao, Te is described throughout the Tao Te Ching. Once we familiarize ourselves with the nature of the Tao, we will be in good shape to understand Te, which is the manifestation of the Tao in human action, reaction and, even, non-action. Those who are close to the Tao are filled with Te. Chapter 21 explains,

Great Te appears flowing from Tao (Addiss).

The Tao Te Ching was written thousands of years ago to teach us how to come close to the Tao and be filled with Te. This lifestyle brings wellbeing to the person and to the cosmos. By abiding by the Tao and acquiring Te, we are able to benefit ourselves and humankind and maintain order and balance in the universe. This is possible by behaving like water, by conducting ourselves in harmony with the Tao, which behaves like water. In Chapter 8, we are taught to,

> Live in a good place.
> Keep your mind deep.
> Treat others well.
> Stand by your word.
> Make fair rules.
> Do the right thing.
> Work when its time.
> Only do not contend,
> And you will not go wrong (Addiss).

A person who can act accordingly - who is cautious, hesitant, polite, yielding, blank, open, and mixes freely (Addiss, 15) - who behaves like water is called a sage. He practices "wu-wei," which literally means non-action, in essence, not to strive, like water, which does not contend. Like the Tao, Te is unfamiliar to most in the West and is difficult to comprehend and, still further, to practice. The sage practices wu-wei and all things in the cosmos settle themselves and return to their natural state; harmony returns to the natural rhythm of the universe and all is restored, as it was meant to be. Wu-wei is not a form of apathy or recklessness. It means to take no unnatural action and to be one with the cosmos, with the Tao, which is "solitary and silent" (Addiss, 25). Understanding this, the world "moves without danger in safety and peace" (Addiss, 35).

Chapter 81 comprehensively and concisely expresses the water-like nature of the Tao in nature and in man:

> Heaven's Tao
> Benefits and does not harm.
> The Sage's Tao
> Acts and does not contend (Addiss).

Wu-wei - acting like water - is well described in chapter 63:

> Do the Non-Ado.
> Strive for the effortless.
> Savor the savorless
> Exalt the low.
> Multiply the few.
> Requite injury with kindness.
> Nip troubles in the bud.
> Sow the great in the small (Wu).

The above passage describes wu-wei on a personal level. Chapter 66, below, describes the sage's wu-wei and its impact on society:

> River and seas
> Can rule the hundred valleys.
> Because they are good at lying low
> They are lords of the valleys.
> Therefore those who would be above
> Must speak as if they are below.
> Those who would lead
> Must speak as if they are behind.
> In this way the sage dwells above
> And the people are not burdened.
> Dwells in front
> And they are not hindered.
> Therefore the whole world
> Is delighted and unwearied.
> Since the Sage does not contend
> No one can contend with the Sage (Addiss).

The sage is praiseworthy as benefactor to universe. Everyone who reads the Tao Te Ching is encouraged to follow the example of the sage, but I do not want my fellow Christians to get the wrong idea. As Christians, we are not meant to emulate the sage - we are meant to emulate Christ. Christ is not the sage. He is not a Taoist. He is the Son of God who mixes up the waters to bring up the poor. He had no desire to leave the world as it was. He came to the earth as an active agent to lift up the weak, the infirm, the poor and the afflicted.

In Chapter 8, we learn,

> Water knows how to benefit all things without striving with them.
> It stays in places loathed by all men.
> Therefore, it comes near to the Tao (Wu).

Of all things, water comes nearest to Tao. They share common qualities and behave in similar manners. Water is essential to life and is our body's most vital nutrient. It nourishes us like the Tao nourishes us. Even though it excels, it does not strive with anything because it voluntarily takes the lowest position, like the man of Tao. Most men seek fame, fortune and power and desire to be on top, but the man of Tao cultivates modesty and humility and chooses the low. Most men loathe the low, when,

> Truly, humility is the root from which greatness springs,
> And the high must be built upon the foundation of the low.
> That is why barons and princes style themselves 'The Helpless One,' 'The Little One,' 'The Worthless One.'
> Perhaps they too realize their dependence upon the lowly.

Truly, too much honor means no honor
(Wu, 39).

Even Christ, our Lord, acknowledging His humanity,
humbles Himself at the title "Good Teacher," when
He says "Why do you call me good? No one is good
but God alone" (Mark 10:18). God humbled Himself
and became man for us. No words can express His
goodness, yet He corrects the rich man for calling
Him good. This is the epitome of humility. This is
what it means to come near to the Tao, like water.

Water into Wine

In the poorest countries, drinkable water is
scarce and, in many cases, evident throughout history,
it has been replaced by wine:

> Wine had a more practical reason in its
> beginning than the mere pleasure of drinking.
> Ancient peoples had little pure water to drink,
> and they learned that alcohol formed by
> fermentation protected fruit juice from
> spoiling. The people who drank this
> fermented juice did not get sick as often as
> those that drank the impure water. This
> reason for wine drinking continues down to
> our day. Many peoples, especially [in poorer
> countries,] use wine [diluted] instead of water

for drinking (The World Book Encyclopedia, 1966, "Wine").

This truth gives us a key insight into our Lord's first sign that revealed He was the Son of God. He turned water into wine, literally, as expressed in the Gospel of John, but just as importantly, He did so in a figurative and celestial sense. The ancient Chinese sages likened the Tao to water and Christ turned the Tao into what can be best described as wine. There was a lack of pure water for the people to drink in that the Tao of the ancient Chinese sages was scarce. It could not help most people because the Tao's lofty esoteric principles were followed by few. So, Christ transformed the Tao into what resembles wine for all people, especially the poor, to quench their thirst, to nourish their souls. Truly, water was made wine. Truly, the Tao was transformed. Truly, Christ came into the world for the poor and afflicted.

In Chapter 23 of the Tao Te Ching, we learn: "those on the way become the way." Christ became the way. "I am the way, and the truth, and the life," He says. He is the new way. His incarnation, ministry, death, resurrection and ascension mark the beginning of a new time. "I make all things new," so His words read and so we have seen since his advent. Only the Son of God could have renewed the Tao.

Christ's first sign that manifested his glory took place at a wedding in Cana:

On the third day there was a marriage at Cana in Galilee, and the mother of Jesus was there; 2 Jesus also was invited to the marriage, with his disciples. 3 When the wine gave out, the mother of Jesus said to him, "They have no wine." 4 And Jesus said to her, "O woman, what have you to do with me? My hour has not yet come." 5 His mother said to the servants, "Do whatever he tells you." 6 Now six stone jars were standing there, for the Jewish rites of purification, each holding twenty or thirty gallons. 7 Jesus said to them, "Fill the jars with water." And they filled them up to the brim. 8 He said to them, "Now draw some out, and take it to the steward of the feast." So they took it. 9 When the steward of the feast tasted the water now become wine, and did not know where it came from (though the servants who had drawn the water knew), the steward of the feast called the bridegroom 10 and said to him, "Every man serves the good wine first; and when men have drunk freely, then the poor wine; but you have kept the good wine until now." 11 This, the first of his signs, Jesus did at Cana in Galilee, and manifested his glory; and his disciples believed in him (John 2:1, RSV).

There are few occasions that can be as joyous as a wedding. It is when two souls become one and it is a time to celebrate a new beginning and a new life. Our Lord chose such a celebration of new beginnings to begin His ministry and because of Him the way of the cosmos would begin new. Turning water into wine showed God's presence in our Lord. In a literal sense, I may not understand the sign, but I believe, I have faith. Skeptics may have doubts, but our Lord performed many signs that are beyond our limited human mind. And this should not be cause for alarm, for there are instances of holy men and women to this day who perform signs pointing to the glory of God that we may not understand. We must not be puffed up with pride and think that we know everything or vain and think too highly of ourselves. And, we should not give too much credit to our faculties of reasoning. Let us remember Plato and his allegory of the cave where men believed in shadows on the wall and how they were unable fathom the realities that were beyond those shadows with the limited scope of their knowledge.

However, if this sign was taken only literally, then we would miss an extremely significant, deep and important symbolic lesson, which is just as potent as the literal lesson. Christ turned water into wine to show us and make us understand the bigger picture. The plain sign of physically turning water into wine helps us to ascertain the celestial transformation of the Tao. Once we realize what our Lord did by transforming the Tao, the plain sign's symbolic meaning is clear and visible; and then we can see how the plain sign clarifies, supports and makes certain the deeper sign of transforming the Tao. The plain sign helps us to conceptualize the deeper sign and it sheds light on the deeper sign. It is an anticipation or prefiguring of the deeper sign. The plain sign teaches a lesson that paves the way for the deeper sign and makes the deeper sign discernible. The two phenomena parallel each other.

Second century Church theologian Melito of Sardis explains,

> Nothing, beloved, is spoken or made without an analogy and a sketch; for everything which is made and spoken has its analogy, what is spoken an analogy, what is made a prototype, so that whatever is made may be perceived through the prototype and whatever is spoken clarified by the illustration (*On Pascha*, 35 [SVS Press book, 46]).

Melito's theology is evident when our Lord transformed water into wine, which foreshadowed the transformation of the Tao. Most noticeable and most important is that Christ acts at the wedding during a time of tribulation - the lack of wine - which is an analogy or "preliminary sketch" of His action as the Savior of the world. Christ makes wine on the third day at the wedding. This sign foreshadowed His Resurrection from the dead on the third day, which was the beginning of the Messianic Wine. On the third day, He saves the wedding and on the third day, He saves the world. Christ's Mother foresees trouble as the wine gives out and notifies her son. "They have no wine," she alerts. He is reluctant to act because His "hour" had not yet come - the time when He was to fulfill His destiny as humankind's Savior from death defined by his glorious Passion and Resurrection. Nonetheless, He acts and so begins a new age for humankind with Christ as our Immortal Priest King.

Very telling are the steward's words about the quality of wine served at the wedding. He says, "Every man serves the good wine first; and when men have drunk freely, then the poor wine; but you have kept the good wine until now." His words are prophetic and poignant. The wine served first was inferior to Christ's wine, which was remarkable and exceptional. The wine served first reached an end just as the Jewish faith was to reach its final day. The Jewish nation proved to be unfruitful. As Prophet Isaiah professed,

> Let me sing for my beloved
>   a love song concerning his vineyard:
> My beloved had a vineyard
>   on a very fertile hill.
> 2 He digged it and cleared it of stones,
>   and planted it with choice vines;
> he built a watchtower in the midst of it,
>   and hewed out a wine vat in it;

and he looked for it to yield grapes,
    but it yielded wild grapes.
3 And now, O inhabitants of Jerusalem
    and men of Judah,
judge, I pray you, between me
    and my vineyard.
4 What more was there to do for my vineyard,
    that I have not done in it?
When I looked for it to yield grapes,
    why did it yield wild grapes?
5 And now I will tell you
    what I will do to my vineyard.
I will remove its hedge,
    and it shall be devoured;
I will break down its wall,
    and it shall be trampled down.
6 I will make it a waste;
    it shall not be pruned or hoed,
    and briers and thorns shall grow up;
I will also command the clouds
    that they rain no rain upon it.
7 For the vineyard of the Lord of hosts
    is the house of Israel,
and the men of Judah
    are his pleasant planting;
and he looked for justice,
    but behold, bloodshed;
for righteousness,
    but behold, a cry! (Isaiah 5:1, RSV).

The Jewish nation protests and pleads to God to save it. In Scripture, we hear,

> Thou didst bring a vine out of Egypt [when the Jews were slaves];
>   thou didst drive out the nations and plant it.
> 9 Thou didst clear the ground for it;
>   it took deep root and filled the land.
> 10 The mountains were covered with its shade,
>   the mighty cedars with its branches;
> 11 it sent out its branches to the sea,
>   and its shoots to the River.
> 12 Why then hast thou broken down its walls,
>   so that all who pass along the way pluck its fruit?
> 13 The boar from the forest ravages it,
>   and all that move in the field feed on it.
> 14 Turn again, O God of hosts!
>   Look down from heaven, and see;
> have regard for this vine,
> 15   the stock which thy right hand planted.[b]
> 16 They have burned it with fire, they have cut it down;
>   may they perish at the rebuke of thy countenance!
> 17 But let thy hand be upon the man of thy right hand,

the son of man whom thou hast made strong
for thyself!
18 Then we will never turn back from thee;
   give us life, and we will call on thy name!
19 Restore us, O Lord God of hosts!
   let thy face shine, that we may be saved!
(Psalm 80:8, RSV).

Christ hears the cry and becomes the above son of
man at the right hand of God who restores and saves
God's people. Christ calls himself the true vine,

"I am the true vine, and my Father is the
vinedresser. 2 Every branch of mine that bears
no fruit, he takes away, and every branch that
does bear fruit he prunes, that it may bear
more fruit. 3 You are already made clean by
the word which I have spoken to you. 4 Abide
in me, and I in you. As the branch cannot bear
fruit by itself, unless it abides in the vine,
neither can you, unless you abide in me. 5 I
am the vine, you are the branches. He who
abides in me, and I in him, he it is that bears
much fruit, for apart from me you can do
nothing. 6 If a man does not abide in me, he is
cast forth as a branch and withers; and the
branches are gathered, thrown into the fire and
burned. 7 If you abide in me, and my words
abide in you, ask whatever you will, and it
shall be done for you. 8 By this my Father is

glorified, that you bear much fruit, and so prove to be my disciples. 9 As the Father has loved me, so have I loved you; abide in my love. 10 If you keep my commandments, you will abide in my love, just as I have kept my Father's commandments and abide in his love. 11 These things I have spoken to you, that my joy may be in you, and that your joy may be full. 12 "This is my commandment, that you love one another as I have loved you. 13 Greater love has no man than this, that a man lay down his life for his friends. 14 You are my friends if you do what I command you. 15 No longer do I call you servants,[a] for the servant[b] does not know what his master is doing; but I have called you friends, for all that I have heard from my Father I have made known to you. 16 You did not choose me, but I chose you and appointed you that you should go and bear fruit and that your fruit should abide; so that whatever you ask the Father in my name, he may give it to you. 17 This I command you, to love one another (John 15:1, RSV).

Christ is the Jewish nation's salvation. He is the only fruitful vine. The Jewish nation failed to produce fruit, so Christ stepped in and took action. The wine that Christ produced is extraordinary and is the awaited celebratory wine of the triumphant Messianic Age.

The massive amount of wine produced - six stone jars each holding twenty or thirty gallons - signifies that in the age of Christ there is enough wine for everybody (insight from Stanley D. Toussaint, "The Significance of the First Sign in John's Gospel," *Bibliotheca Sacra*, (Jan-Mar 1977): 49-51).

Christ's first sign is an "analogy" or "preliminary sketch" for the transformation of the Tao. He performed His first sign with water because it best characterized the Tao and the Taoist sages, too, identified water as the best expression of the Tao. Both Jewish Christ and the Taoists sages saw the Tao in the same way. I believe that there are universal truths and that religions often illustrate these truths with common metaphors, such as light, darkness and fire. So, when Christ transformed water into wine - symbolically announcing the impact He was going to have on the cosmos - He used the same expression as the Taoist sages and equated water with the Tao. For both Jewish Christ and the Taoist sages, the cosmos's natural rhythm was best described as "the waters above the heavens." It is a shared metaphor. Both Taoists and Christ observed a common truth. Such theology is also seen when Christ allegorizes his body with the temple (John 2:19). Christ calls his body a temple in the same way that Buddhists call the body a temple. It is a shared metaphor. There is shared theology among religions as well as in their metaphors.

The new wine in Christ's first sign represents the Messianic Age. Jewish Scripture often uses wine to describe the Messianic Age. From Prophet Joel, we learn,

> And in that day
> the mountains shall drip sweet wine,
>   and the hills shall flow with milk,
> and all the stream beds of Judah
>   shall flow with water (Joel 3:18, RSV).

The image of a vineyard and an abundance of wine marking the Messianic Age is clearly painted by Prophet Amos, in whom God speaks and declares,

> "Behold, the days are coming," says the Lord,
>   "when the plowman shall overtake the reaper
>   and the treader of grapes him who sows the seed;
> the mountains shall drip sweet wine,
>   and all the hills shall flow with it.
> 14 I will restore the fortunes of my people Israel,
>   and they shall rebuild the ruined cities and inhabit them;
> they shall plant vineyards and drink their wine,

and they shall make gardens and eat their
fruit (Amos 9:13, RSV).

The promise of the Messianic Age came to fruition
with our Lord. This coming age was already present
in Christ who performed signs trumpeting His arrival
as the sovereign ruler of the Jewish nation. By
transforming water into wine, He made Himself
known and thereby begins a new age, with a new
cosmic order in which Christ our Lord is King and
God.

The Messianic Age began with Christ because
of Christ. The workings of the Holy Spirit define the
Messianic Age. Christ gave sight to the blind, healed
the lame, cleansed the lepers and cast out demons.
God had pity on us and sent His Incarnate Son to
renew our fallen state. Action was necessary. The
cosmic order which was once maintained by non-
action, as prescribed by the ancient Chinese sages,
was transformed by God through His Incarnate Son
for the salvation of man. The selfless proactive action
of Christ was the new Way, the new Tao. When
Christ was on the Cross and His work on earth was
complete, He gave up the Holy Spirit. Prior to His
death, He told His disciples, "I tell you the truth: it is
to your advantage that I go away, for if I do not go
away, the Counselor [Holy Spirit] will not come to
you; but if I go, I will send him to you" (John 16:7,
RSV). This promise was fulfilled after Christ's
crucifixion at Pentecost when the Holy Spirit entered

the Apostles and they were given the power to perform God's signs in the name of Christ:

> When the day of Pentecost had come, they were all together in one place. 2 And suddenly a sound came from heaven like the rush of a mighty wind, and it filled all the house where they were sitting. 3 And there appeared to them tongues as of fire, distributed and resting on each one of them. 4 And they were all filled with the Holy Spirit and began to speak in other tongues, as the Spirit gave them utterance.
> ... 12 And all were amazed and perplexed, saying to one another, "What does this mean?" 13 But others mocking said, "They are filled with new wine."
> 14 But Peter, standing with the eleven, lifted up his voice and addressed them, "Men of Judea and all who dwell in Jerusalem, let this be known to you, and give ear to my words. 15 For these men are not drunk, as you suppose, since it is only the third hour of the day; 16 but this is what was spoken by the prophet Joel:

> > 17 'And in the last days it shall be, God declares,
> > that I will pour out my Spirit upon all flesh,

and your sons and your daughters shall
prophesy,
and your young men shall see visions,
and your old men shall dream dreams;
18 yea, and on my menservants and
my maidservants in those days
I will pour out my Spirit; and they
shall prophesy.
19 And I will show wonders in the
heaven above
and signs on the earth beneath,
blood, and fire, and vapor of smoke;
20 the sun shall be turned into
darkness
and the moon into blood,
before the day of the Lord comes,
the great and manifest day.
21 And it shall be that whoever calls
on the name of the Lord shall be
saved' (Acts 2:1, RSV).

Most telling is how the onlookers believed that the
disciples were "filled with new wine." Indeed, they
were. They were filled with new wine - the wine of
the Holy Spirit. They were not drunk from a liquid,
but moved from within by the Holy Spirit, who is the
essence of the Messianic Age. The new Tao of Christ
had come upon the earth and was made manifest in
the disciples at Pentecost.

The new Tao of Christ and the Messianic Age was revealed by Christ when He preached the Sermon on the Mount. Most poignant are the Beatitudes, the Blessings:

"Blessed are the poor in spirit, for theirs is the kingdom of heaven.

4 "Blessed are those who mourn, for they shall be comforted.

5 "Blessed are the meek, for they shall inherit the earth.

6 "Blessed are those who hunger and thirst for righteousness, for they shall be satisfied.

7 "Blessed are the merciful, for they shall obtain mercy.

8 "Blessed are the pure in heart, for they shall see God.

9 "Blessed are the peacemakers, for they shall be called sons of God.

10 "Blessed are those who are persecuted for righteousness' sake, for theirs is the kingdom of heaven.

11 "Blessed are you when men revile you and persecute you and utter all kinds of evil against you falsely on my account. 12 Rejoice and be glad, for your reward is great in heaven, for so men persecuted the prophets who were before you (Matthew 5:3, RSV).

In the Sermon on the Mount, Christ preached a new message, a revolutionary message that transformed the world. He preached the Gospel, the Good News, the coming of God's Kingdom of Heaven for all people - including the weak, the infirm, the poor and the afflicted. A taste of Heaven has come upon the earth for those who live by Christ's teachings. And Paradise - a place of bliss in God's Supreme Love - awaits those who repent for their sins and pray for mercy. Because of God's merciful Grace, eternal life awaits those who seek it and journey toward it.

Christ has unveiled the mysteries of Heaven and Hell. God has made Christ Judge, so justice and righteousness may prevail. Miracles - God's works - have manifested on earth. Saints have walked the earth performing signs and healing the sick.

Salvation is awarded to those who "love the Lord your God with all your heart, and with all your soul, and with all your mind" and those who "love your neighbor as yourself" (Matthew 22:37-39, RSV).

Love - specifically, agape love - is the key to God's Kingdom of Heaven and Paradise. The commandment to be filled with agape love is exemplified by Christ who suffered for us on the Cross. He paid the ultimate price and gave up His life because He loved us so much. As the Tao Te Ching teaches, "Extreme love exacts a great price" (Addiss, 44). Christ's agape love is the new way that forever changed the cosmos.

In this treatise, we have dug deep into invaluable treasures and have uncovered hidden truths. As the Son of God, Christ transformed water into wine at a wedding in Cana in Galilee. This sign foreshadowed and illustrated His transformation of the Tao - a feat that only the Son of God could have performed. The ancient Chinese sages used the term Tao to refer to the natural rhythm of the cosmos and they observed that it behaved like water. The Tao's lofty esoteric principles were followed by few. But, there was tribulation in the world and Christ came into the world to save all people, not just the few. He transformed the Tao into what resembles wine to save lowly humankind from its sins. With the supreme transformation of the Tao, Christ ushered in a new cosmic order and announced to the world His eminence as Lord, King and God.

TREATISE TWO

AGAPE INTO ETERNITY

JAMES THOMAS ANGELIDIS

PART ONE

UNION WITH GOD

Hindu theology was fundamental as I worked out my understanding of God, the universe and us. The *Upanishads* and *Bhagavad-Gita* are the two most revered Hindu texts and were of principal importance during my quest for answers. They are the result of the human inquiry, but go beyond philosophy to become revelation. I wanted to know the meaning and goal of life, so I went to the literature that disclosed or at least, thought deeply about them. There are countless numbers of books that have passed the test of time, but few books have thrived as perennially as the *Upanishads* and *Bhagavad-Gita.* There are a couple of hundred Upanishads, but the first twenty or so are the most significant and they date back as far as 3000 years ago. The sages who authored them are some of the first to ponder human existence and to this very day, hundreds of millions of Hindus abide by their teachings. This attests to the strength of their claims. The *Bhagavad-Gita* stems from the *Upanishads* and seems to have begun to take form as far back as 2500 years ago. Hindus of all walks of life treasure the *Bhagavad-Gita* as a transformative masterpiece. It would be foolish to object to their teachings without examining them, so I encourage all to read them. You will be surprised with how refreshing they are.

The two most important words in the *Upanishads* and *Bhagavad-Gita* are Brahman and Atman. These are no ordinary words because their meanings cannot be confined to word definitions. Brahman is that "which cannot be expressed in words but by which the tongue speaks - know that to be Brahman... That which is not comprehended by the mind, but by which the mind comprehends - know that to be Brahman... That which is not seen by the eye but by which the eye sees - know that to be Brahman... That which is not heard by the ear but by which the ear hears - know that to be Brahman... That which is not drawn by the breath but by which the breath is drawn - know that to be Brahman (Kena, Upanishads, Signet Classic, 30). Nonetheless, the ancient Hindu sages explain that Brahman is the supreme infinite reality of the universe. It is the origin: "Brahman willed that it should be so, and brought forth out of himself the material cause of the universe; from this came the primal energy, and from the primal energy mind, from mind the subtle elements, from the subtle elements the many worlds, and from the acts performed by beings in the many worlds the chain of cause and effect - the reward and punishment of works" (Mundaka, Upanishads, 43). The "self-luminous, subtler than the subtlest, in whom exist all the worlds and all those that live therein - he is the imperishable Brahman. He is the principle of life. He is speech, and he is mind. He is real. He is immortal. Attain him, O my friend, the one goal to be attained! (Mundaka, Upanishads, 45).

Atman is the innermost reality of a person. "When we consider Brahman as lodged within the individual being, we call Him Atman" (Bhagavad-Gita, Signet Classic, 74). Atman is within and Brahman is without. Atman is Brahman and Brahman is all (Isha, Upanishads, 26) "This Atman, who understands all, who knows all, and whose glory is manifest in the universe, lives within the lotus of the heart, the bright throne of Brahman. By the pure in heart is he known. The Atman exists in man, within the lotus of the heart, and is the master of his life and of his body. With mind illumined by the power of meditation, the wise know him, the blissful, the immortal" (Mundaka, Upanishads, 46). "The Atman is ear of the ear, mind of the mind, speech of speech. He is also breath of the breathe, and eye of the eye. Having given up the false identification of the Atman with the senses and the mind, and knowing the Atman to be Brahman, the wise, on departing this life, become immortal" (Kena, Upanishads, 30).

Brahman is the universe's soul and Atman is the individual's soul and they are of the same essence and substance. Atman within is immortal, like Brahman without. Life's purpose is to release and free Atman, so it may become one with Brahman. When Atman becomes one with Brahman, the devotee transcends suffering and death and becomes immortal. It is like when a drop of water enters and becomes one with water. To become one with the immortal is to become immortal. "Let him worship Brahman as Brahman, and he will become Brahman" (Taittiriya, Upanishads, 59). "When can a man be said to have achieved union with Brahman? When his mind is under perfect control and freed from all desires, so that he becomes absorbed in the Atman, and nothing else" (Bhagavad-Gita, 66). The devotee's "mind is dead to the touch of the external: it is alive to the bliss of the Atman. Because his heart knows Brahman his happiness is forever" (Bhagavad-Gita, 60). The sages, "these great ones attain to immortality in this very life; and when their bodies fall away from them at death, they attain liberation" (Mundaka, Upanishads, 48). "The secret of immortality is to be found in purification of the heart, in meditation, in realization of the identity of the Atman within and the Brahman without. For immortality is union with God" (Katha, Upanishads, 13).

However, uniting Atman with Brahman takes effort because we are consumed by other concerns. The ancient Hindu sages understood that the world is filled with suffering and our suffering is caused by our worldly attachments and actions. We work for riches, fame, sex and power, but our actions are futile because those things fail to satisfy. "Thinking about-sense objects will attach you to sense-objects; grow attached, and you become addicted; thwart your addiction, it turns to anger; be angry, and you confuse your mind; confuse your mind, you forget the lesson of experience; forget experience, you lose discrimination; lose discrimination, and you miss life's only purpose" (Bhagavad-Gita, 42). "He who, brooding upon sense objects, comes to yearn for them, is born here and there, again and again, driven by his desire. But he who has realized the Atman, and thus satisfied all hunger, attains to liberation even in this life" (Mundaka, Upanishads, 48). Our actions have held Atman, within, hostage. You "must first control your senses, then kill this evil thing which obstructs discriminative knowledge and realization of the Atman (Bhagavad-Gita, 49). Through self-discipline, asceticism and mysticism, we can detach ourselves from worldly attachments, break free from the confines of the world and transcend suffering and death. The release, liberation and emancipation from suffering, the world and death is called Moksha.

The relationship between Brahman and Atman reveals deep truths about the relationship between God and us. This Hindu theology is also sound Christian theology. The following verse is a part of the ancient Trisagion Prayer, which many Orthodox Christian's use daily:

> O heavenly King, O Comforter, the Spirit of truth, who art in all places and fillest all things; Treasury of good things and Giver of life: Come and dwell in us and cleanse us

from every stain, and save our souls, O
gracious Lord (*A Pocket Prayer Book for
Orthodox Christians*, Antiochian Orthodox
Christian Archdiocese of North America
1956, 5).

This simple, yet powerful prayer is an excellent
representation of a shared theology between Hindus
and Christians. I have recited this prayer twice a day
- once in the morning and once at night - for nearly
ten years. My journey through the great world
religions' sacred scriptures began over ten years ago.
The shared theology that I discovered had been with
me for a while, but one night, as I was reciting the
prayer, I made the connection between the prayer and
the theology. That ordinary day turned into an
extraordinary night because the theology I discovered
was confirmed. It was crystallized in this prayer. I
knew the theology was correct, but the prayer
expressed it perfectly. The prayer's words are few,
but its theology is eternal. The next day, I told a
coworker who is a friend and later that day, I told my
parents that I was able to describe the means to
Heaven and immortality. I was talking so quickly
that they encouraged me to breath. I could barely
sleep for four days and I did not want to sleep. My
eyes were as wide as the moon and my spirit
ascended to the heavens. Peace filled my soul and I
knew I had to express my discovery so others could
understand it. In this work, I hope I have done so. I

wish I was a better writer, communicator and teacher, but here, I have done my best. In a moment, I will illustrate how love - specifically, agape love - is important to this cosmic theology. As the theology has done for me, I believe it will bring hope, comfort and peace to many in our troubled world.

To make clear the prayer's theology, I have broken it down below:

- O heavenly King, O Comforter, the Spirit of truth, who art in all places and fillest all things [the definition of Brahman]

- Treasury of good things and Giver of life: Come and dwell in us [the definition Atman]

- and cleanse us from every stain, and save our souls [the definition of Moksha]

- O gracious Lord.

This is a prayer from a Christian to Almighty God, but it can easily be used by a Hindu to pray to Almighty Brahman. It reveals the relationship between God and us - the Creator and the created - and our deep desire for Salvation - the means to union with Him - which is only possible because of His Grace.

In the same way that Hindu's believe Atman is Brahman and Brahman is all, Christians believe Jesus is God and God is all. Hindu's believe Atman is true Brahman of true Brahman and Christians believe Jesus is true God of true God. In the same way that Hindus believe Atman is one essence and substance of Brahman who is the source all things, Christians believe Jesus is of one essence with God, by whom all things were made. In the same way that Hindus believe that Atman is the true self and the full potential of the individual known only by the pure in heart, the Apostle Paul says, "it is no longer I who live, but Christ who lives in me" (Galatians 2:20).

Hindu's believe union with Brahman is made possible through Moksha and Christians believe union with God is made possible through Salvation. The theology is similar, but not the same. Moksha leads to complete satisfaction, fullness and peace; while, Salvation leads to unmitigated bliss. Hindus believe that discriminative knowledge through self-discipline makes Moksha possible; while, Christians believe agape love makes Salvation possible. The difference between discriminative knowledge and agape love is the difference between satisfaction and bliss.

As I was studying the Christian Bible's New Testament, I discovered a powerful insight that struck me and deepened my understanding about God. That is, "God is agape" (1 John 4:8). Christianity is the only religion to make this claim. Here, we learn that not only does God have agape for us, He is Agape. In the next chapter, I will define agape in detail, but for now, it is enough to know that agape means love - the kind of love Jesus embodied.

Agape is crucial for union with God. There are many ways to get close to God, but only agape can unite us with God. God is the source of agape and God's Son Jesus brings God's agape to earth. Jesus is agape Incarnate and perfectly revealed agape to the world through his life, suffering and death. To become one with God, we must become one with the Son. Becoming one with the Son is the only way to become one with God because the Son fills us with agape and only those who are filled with agape can become one with God who is Agape. To be filled with agape, we have to be reborn in spirit with God's Son Jesus. We do not know agape or how to give agape until Jesus enters us. It begins with respect and recognition of his suffering. Consider his suffering and it will lead to empathy. Agape compelled him and his agape will fill you with agape. Then, you will understand that he was no ordinary man. He will transform your mind and heart. And, when you pay attention to his teachings, you will hear truth in his words. No man spoke like this man. No man died like this man. No man loved like this man. Reflect and embrace him and you will understand why Christians call him God's Suffering Servant, the Christ and God's Son.

Jesus's agape lives within us and God's agape lives all around us. The purpose of life is to unite the agape within us with the agape all around us - in the

same way that a drop of water becomes one with
water. Those who can - like the saints - attain
immortality.

Like the Hindu sages who wrote the
Upanishads, Jesus believed that oneness with God is
the Ultimate. In prayer, he asks his Father, "I do not
pray for these [his disciples] only, but also for those
who believe in me through their word, that they may
all be one; even as thou, Father, art in me, and I in
thee, that they also may be in us, so that the world
may believe that thou hast sent me. The glory which
thou hast given me I have given to them, that they
may be one even as we are one, I in them and thou in
me, that they may become perfectly one" (John
17:20). This way, Jesus explains, "the world may
know that thou hast sent me and hast loved them even
as thou hast loved me." Jesus wants the world to
know about the love he and his Father have for each
other and that the Father loves those who follow Jesus
as much as He loves Jesus.

Jesus tells us, "As the Father has loved me, so
have I loved you; abide in my love" (John 15:9). The
agape Jesus has with his Father he wants us to have
with him. He wants us to have the same relationship
with him as he has with his Father. God and Jesus's
relationship is no ordinary relationship because they
are not ordinary. They are perfect and their agape is
perfect. There is no agape more sublime or glorious
than the agape between the Father and the Son. An
agape of the highest order from "before the

foundation of the world" (John 17:24). Jesus invites us to be a part of their agape. Could anything be better? Who would not want to join God and His Son and their agape? At the nadir of human history, when Jesus was sacrificed, their agape remained irrepressible and undying. Like at the highest of highests, at the lowest of lowests, their love is perfection. Through them we are saved. "For God so loved the world that He gave his only Son, that whoever believes in him should not perish but have eternal life" (John 3:16). Because of their love for each other and us, the angels sing, "Hallelujah, Hallelujah, Hallelujah! Glory to You O God!" Their agape for each other conquered death and Jesus wants us to abide in that same agape with him, so we, too, can conquer death.

Jesus tells us, "If you keep my commandments, you will abide in my love, just as I have kept my Father's commandments and abide in his love" (John 15:10). Keeping Jesus's commandments means embodying agape as he does. If my master was an ordinary man and he told me that he would love me if I kept his commandments, I would be skeptical, even apprehensive. His commandments may be outrageous. However, Jesus does not command us with rules or laws. He works on what is within us. Jesus's commandments have to do with agape: "You shall love the Lord your God with all your heart, and with all your soul, and with all your mind. This is the great and first commandment. And a second is like it, You shall love your neighbor as yourself" (Matthew 22:37). Loving God and neighbor will move us to bring Heaven to earth. A time and place when and where, "the mountains shall drip sweet wine, and the hills shall flow with milk, and all the stream beds of Judah shall flow with water" (Joel 3:18). Jesus even tells us, "Love your enemies and pray for those who persecute you... For if you love those who love you, what reward have you? Do not even the tax collectors do the same? And if you salute only your brethren, what more are you doing than others? Do not even the Gentiles do the same?" (Matthew 5:44). By keeping Jesus's commandments, we will abide in his love, just as he has kept his Father's commandments and abides in His love. To "abide in" means to remain or dwell in. To abide in agape is to dwell in a state, place or being that is agape. When Jesus abides in God's agape, he dwells in God's agape and is one with God. Jesus invites us to dwell in his agape just as he dwells in God's agape. Agape unites God and Jesus and agape unites Jesus and us. How comforting is that? Irresistible, indeed, to know that agape is the only thing necessary to unite us with God and Jesus. Agape is all you need.

There is a special relationship among the Father, the Son and us. Jesus tells us, "I am in my Father, and you in me, and I in you" (John 14:20b). We who keeps Jesus's commandments of agape are in Jesus and because Jesus is in the Father we, too, are in the Father. Jesus also tells us that he is in us. We who are filled with agape like Jesus have Jesus in us. As Apostle Paul said, "it is no longer I who live, but Christ who lives in me" (Galatians 2:20). Through agape, we can be one with Jesus and because Jesus is "Light of Light, true God of true God," we can be one with God. Because of Jesus, we can be in God and God in us. Thus, we are one with God. Jesus, who is inside us, is the same essence as God, who is greater than the universe. This relationship is identical to the Hindu theology that the Atman inside of us is the same essence as Brahman, who is greater than the universe.

In prayer, Jesus asks his Father, "the love with which thou hast loved me may be in them, and I in them" (John 17:26). This agape from God and Jesus that Jesus prays for us to have inside of us is like the Hindu Atman. Hindus teach that Atman "lives within the lotus of the heart, the bright throne of Brahman" (Mundaka, Upanishads, 46). Similarly, God who is greater than the universe has a place in our hearts. There is a place for Almighty God in our hearts, if we let him in.

Jesus tells us, "If a man loves me, he will keep my word, and my Father will love him, and we will come to him and make our home with him" (John 14:23). If we love Jesus, God will love us and we will live in agape with God and Jesus forever together in their home in Heaven - a place where the King is known as a Comforter and rules with his Spirit and speaks Truth.

Jesus tells us, "These things I have spoken to you, that my joy may be in you, and that your joy may be full" (John 15:11). And, he tells us, "The word which you hear is not mine but the Father's who sent me" (John 14:24b).

The author of 1 John speaks to us saying, "Beloved, let us love [agape] one another; for love is of God, and he who loves is born of God and knows God. He who does not love does not know God; for God is love. In this love of God was made manifest among us, that God sent his only Son into the world, so that we might live through him. In this is love, not that we loved God but that he loved us and sent his Son to be the expiation for our sins. Beloved, if God so loved us, we also ought to love one another. No man has ever seen God; if we love one another, God abides in us and his love is perfected in us. By this we know that we abide in him and he in us, because he has given us of his own Spirit. And we have seen and testify that the Father has sent his Son as the Savior of the world. Whoever confesses that Jesus is the Son of God, God abides in him, and he in God. So we know and believe the love God has for us. God is love, and he who abides in love abides in God, and God abides in him. In this is love perfected with us, that we may have confidence for the day of judgment, because as he is so are we in this world. There is no fear in love, but perfect love casts out fear. For fear has to do with punishment, and he who fears is not perfected in love. We love, because he first loved us. If any one says, "I love God," and hates his brother, he is a liar; for he who does not love his brother whom he has seen, cannot love God whom he has not seen. And this commandment we have from him, that he who loves God should love his brother also (1 John 4:7).

In Hinduism, when a devotee's Atman is one with Brahman, the devotee is perfect and is destined for immortality. Similarly, in Christianity, when a Christian "confesses that Jesus is the Son of God, God abides in him, and he in God." If God is in the Christian and the Christian is in God, the Christian is one with God. This union with God is life's goal because it means immortality. Furthermore, "God is love, and he who abides in love abides in God, and God abides in him." God is agape and the Christian who dwells in agape dwells in God and God dwells in him. "In this is love perfected with us." Such a one who is united with God through agape is destined for immortality. The agape we share with God must be shared with one another. "[If] we love one another, God abides in us and his love is perfected in us. By this we know that we abide in him and he in us, because he has given us of his own Spirit." Those who do not have agape in them should fear the day of judgement. One who rejects agape has rejected God. Therefore, Salvation would be meaningless and impossible. However, we must not be quick to judge each other. We do not know what is in another's heart, if one has made a home for God in one's soul. Only God knows and He will judge us according to our agape.

PART TWO

DEFINING AGAPE LOVE

The ancient Greeks identified four forms of love that we experience in life: storge, philia, eros, agape. Before Jesus, the term agape was rarely used because it was so general. The other terms for love had specific meanings - storge refers to love for family, philia refers to love for friends, eros refers to love for a romantic partner - which allowed one to express more clearly what one wanted to say. Christians adopted the general term agape and revolutionized it to indicate Jesus and Christians' unique love. After Jesus, when people heard the term agape, they understood it meant Christian love (Kreeft, *The God Who Loves You*, 50).

Jesus defines agape because in his life and death, he expresses its meaning in totality. In life, Jesus taught us how to have agape: "love the Lord your God with all your heart, and with all your soul, and with all your mind [and] love your neighbor as yourself" (Matthew 22:37). And, in death, Jesus showed us how to have agape: "By this we know love, that he [Jesus] laid down his life for us; and we ought to lay down our lives for the brethren" (1 John 3:16). Jesus's message and death are the perfect expressions of agape.

Agape is the essence of our relationship with God. His agape is a gift to us because He does not need to love us. We are blessed that He has agape for us and that He considers us. Just as He did not need to create Creation, He does not need to give us the gift of agape. However, just as He created light and earth and man and saw that they were good, He showers us with agape and sees that it is good. God created us because He wanted to and He gives us His gift of agape because He wants to. Furthermore, God created just so He could share agape with Creation. God has agape for everything He made, but He does not have agape for everything in the same way. We are special because God made us in His image and likeness and He has so much agape for us that He wants for us what He wants for Himself, which is to live in agape. That was the intention of our existence. We were made to live in Paradise in forever-present agape and though it is now lost, we are, nonetheless, meant to return to Paradise in forever-present agape.

God needs nothing. He has everything. But, there is one thing He desires: our agape. He has given us free will and we can chose Him or not and when a person chooses God, nothing brings God greater happiness. How sweet it is to know that we can make God happy! All was not for nothing. The

Divine Plan has come to fruition. The made has returned to his Maker. God desires for us to have agape for Him in return because He knows the agape shared between He and us will bring us joy, which we know to be true from the testimonies of the saints.

God's agape is evident throughout human history. However, many may say that, at times, God has acted with vengeance and not agape. Many may say that if Jesus was, in fact, His Son, Jesus's sacrifice was the epitome of God's terrible acts. Many may say that Christians are crazy to believe that a God who sacrifices His only Son loves His Son. But, we Christians are not crazy, "For God so loved the world that he gave his only Son, that whoever believes in him [God's Son] should not perish but have eternal life" (John 3:16). God tells me, "Believe in my Son who I love because His death is not the end. His sacrifice was for you because I love you. I love you so much that my Son and I paid the ultimate price with His death. So, do not let Our act of love be in vain. Do not turn away from it. Look at my Son. Believe in Him and we will be together forever in agape." A Christian must have faith in this to be a Christian and if you do, you will see God's agape in everything and everywhere. The sacrifice is real and that is why saints cry with joy - something many may not understand, but which the saints know to be more real than life itself because it arises from deep within their souls - because no love is greater than the agape of God and His Son.

I know God by what I have learned in Scripture and the Church and what is corroborated deep inside my soul. God's agape is real, but many question Him because of tragedies like the 2004 South Asian tsunami and the 2012 Sandy Hook elementary school massacre. Scripture teaches us,

> For my thoughts are not your thoughts,
>   neither are your ways my ways, says the Lord.
> 9 For as the heavens are higher than the earth,
>   so are my ways higher than your ways
>   and my thoughts than your thoughts (Isaiah 55:8).

I trust Scripture and believe what it tells me. I may not know why certain things happen. Many things are beyond me. God's ways are higher than my ways, but I trust God. I believe in His agape and His Son Jesus's agape. When Jesus tells me, "in my Father's house are many rooms," and that he must die and go to his Father to prepare a place for those who follow him, I believe him (John 14:2). I believe in Paradise and that there are rooms for those who follow Jesus in God's house in Paradise.

There have been moments when I have asked myself, "Why do good people suffer misfortune? Where is God when there is pain?" In Scripture, there is a parable about how God gave the homeless Lazarus - whose sores were licked by stray dogs -

relief and eternal peace after death in Paradise. I believe God is good and just and that righteousness will prevail, even if it must be after death. As I dig deep, I hear Jesus cry out to me and to those suffering in this life in this world, "I know your pain!" because he took the form of a human being in flesh and experienced the peak of human suffering by being nailed to a cross for hours and left to die - a torture reserved for criminals, not something we would imagine for the Sinless One. And, to those who have lost loved ones in their lives, to parents who have lost their children (perhaps, life's greatest ill), God cries out to them, "I know your pain!" because His only Son was tortured and killed. Understanding this about Jesus the Christ and God the Father, I find comfort because I know I am not alone. If God and His Son experienced pain, we are not immune to it either.

I believe God never leaves us, even when we think He has. This sentiment is illustrated in one of my favorite poems, *Footprints in the Sand.* In it, a man has a dream about his life with God of which is represented by two sets of footprints on a beach. He notices that during his most difficult times, there is only one set and so questions God's presence. The poem ends with God comforting and reassuring the man that when he saw only one set of footprints on the beach, it was not that God was not by his side, but rather that God was carrying him.

Agape has no motive, other than to give love. It is altruistic and gives without consideration for itself - even in danger. It is resilient and strong, but is gentle. It is gracious. It does not measure or contend. It loves without bias, impartially, disinterestedly and, therefore, is limitless in its love. It loves everyone without reservation. It is unconditional. Its love is absolute. It is the purest of the loves. It does not go wrong because it makes no judgments. It simply loves. It does so without reward because it is its own reward. The more it gives, the more it enjoys. It loves to love. Who can resist such love? For how long can one deny such love? It is free and the most valuable thing in the universe. To deny it to the end is self-destruction because there is no love in the beloved who cannot open himself up to it. Without love, there is no living because to love is to live. To not love only leads to death. Agape is tall, but does not look down on the beloved; rather, it picks the beloved up.

Agape is everlasting because it comes from God. The other forms of love promise to be everlasting and when they are at their peaks, it is easy to believe them, but they do not follow through. My family's storge, my friends' philia and my girlfriends' eros deeply affected me and bettered my life, but the feelings I shared with them were confined by time and space and eventually faded. The power of agape endures. Even when it feels weak because God seems distant, I know it is there because I know God will never leave me. It is faith, but it is not blind faith. I trust Scripture, the Church and the testimonies of the saints who encourage me to stay strong and be patient because God is near. My storge for my family, my philia for my friends and my eros for the girls in my life have faded in time, but my agape for them has not. My agape for them remains in me. It is my moments of agape with them that make me smile during the day and help me sleep soundly at night. The agape I share with them is everlasting because its source is God. God gives us His agape, which we must reciprocate and also share with our neighbor. Even when we behave unlovable, agape remains. Differences and disagreements may tarnish storge, philia and eros, but they will not tarnish agape. Agape is so pure that it does not get dirty.

Agape is unlike the other loves because it is not an emotion - it is an action. Storge, philia and eros are manifested by feelings and become emotions; while, agape is manifested by the will and becomes an action. When our agape is directed toward God, it is a response to and reciprocation of His agape. This is not rooted in a feeling. It is us accepting Him as our Maker. We are His and there is no better way to express our agape for him than to obey His commandments. We express our agape for Jesus in the same way. As Jesus tells us, "He who has my commandments and keeps them, he it is who loves me" (John 14:21). Agape begins with a choice, but it only becomes real if we follow through with action.

It is a love to live by and is not sentimental or romantic.

Agape is not an emotion like happiness. Though its aim is not happiness, if we have agape for God, we will be happy. If we work for happiness and not God, we will never find happiness. If we want happiness, we must not seek happiness, but God who will give us happiness. God knows our agape. There is no fooling Him and He gives happiness to those who love Him for Himself and not to those who seek after what He can give them. Agape is choosing God above all other things. No bond or love is stronger because it is the made returning to his Maker.

When our agape is directed to our neighbors, we are loving God. By loving that which our Maker made, we show our love for our Maker. Out of love for God, we must love our neighbor, who God loves. Jesus calls us brethren: "Truly, I say to you, as you did it to one of the least of these my brethren, you did it to me" (Matthew 25:40). We must follow Jesus's example and love one another: "even as I have loved you, that you also love one another. By this all men will know that you are my disciples, if you have love for one another." (John 13:34). Because of our agape for each other, we are Christians. Agape defines true Christians. Christianity was formed to spread agape. When used correctly, it is the religion of agape. Though storge, philia and eros are noble, agape is divine.

Agape is an activity because God is active. It is alive because God is alive. I have a connection to and relationship with God through the agape. We communicate through agape. Our agape is between the two of us alone together with no one else. It is personal and intimate. God is always awake; He never sleeps and it is up to us to be alert and reciprocate with agape and make the effort to continue the relationship.

Agape and faith are the New Testament's dominant themes and they have a unique relationship. Each has the ability to lead to the other. Through faith in Jesus, one comes to realize the power of agape. Jesus's self-sacrificial death is the ultimate expression of agape. If one has faith in Jesus, one cannot help to follow Jesus's lead and practice agape. Once a believer begins to emulate his Lord by practicing agape - as every believer should - he will become a more fervent believer and a more devoted servant. Faith in Jesus leads to acts of agape. The other direction of the relationship is also true: agape leads to faith. As one begins to practice agape with his neighbor, he will realize the truth of Jesus's message of agape. The more he practices agape, the closer he will be to Jesus. Agape can take one to the threshold of faith and if one continues to follow the path of agape and recognizes the reality of agape's transformative power, his immersion into faith in God and Jesus is not far.

The agape we experience with God is not unlike the eros we experience with a beloved. Both are euphoric and transcendent. Both are unmistakable and transformative. Both take us to places unseen and rise in us feelings never before felt. There is no earthly feeling as powerful as eros, but agape is heavenly. And, still further, the agape we experience with God on earth is only a taste of the unmitigated, fully revealed and eternal agape that we will experience with God in Heaven.

"Greater love [agape] has no man than this,
that a man lay down his life for his friends"
- Jesus
(John 15:13)

Jesus's Passion is the most well documented, detailed and thorough period described in all four Gospels: Matthew, Mark, Luke, John. The term "passion" that is used when we refer to Jesus's Passion does not have the same definition as the term that we use in ordinary daily dialogue. In ordinary daily dialogue, the term passion refers to zeal, love and devotion for person, place, thing or idea. It is true that Jesus was filled with passion, but that is not why we say the Passion of the Christ. The word "passion" comes from a Greek word meaning "to suffer." To suffer means to go through pain, to hurt, to feel close to death, but many not understand the glory of suffering. Suffering brings us closer to Jesus who suffered. With suffering, we have the honor of emulating Jesus - God's only begotten Son - who suffered because of his agape for us. He lowered himself to reach us, so when we die, we can be elevated to be with him.

The Christian Church celebrates Jesus's Passion during Holy Week, which begins with Palm Sunday. For Christians, it is one of the most joyful days of the year, preceded by only Easter and Christmas. It commemorates Jesus's triumphal entry into Jerusalem trumpeting his arrival as our King, Savior and God. He enters the city sitting on a donkey announcing that he is the king that Jerusalem had been waiting for. Prophet Zechariah prophesied;

> Rejoice greatly, O daughter of Zion!
>   Shout aloud, O daughter of Jerusalem!
> Lo, your king comes to you;
>   triumphant and victorious is he,
> humble and riding on an ass,
>   on a colt the foal of an ass (Zechariah 9:9).

The crowd that greeted Jesus glorified him shouting, "Hosanna! Blessed is he who comes in the name of the Lord! Blessed is the kingdom of our father David that is coming! Hosanna in the highest!" (Mark 11:9b). They spread palm tree branches on the ground and hailed him as their King. In the past, on the day before Palm Sunday, I have gone to church and joined fellow Christians to make palm leaf crosses. We split palm leaves into thin strips and then folded them into crosses, which would be handed to the church parishioners the next day on Palm Sunday. I would keep the cross I received all year - sometimes more than a year - because I felt its holy power would bless me.

For Christians, Palm Sunday is a day to celebrate, but the days following Palm Sunday are sad because we know that our King will soon be killed. Jesus is better than a political king who can gain territory or peace for his subjects in this world. He is our King and Priest who can save us from death and give us eternal life. Most did not understand this at first. Not even Jesus's disciples were fully aware of his eternal power. Not until Jesus rose from the dead and appeared to his disciples, did they fully understand his power. Truly, his kingship is not of this world. Jesus's reign is in the Kingdom of God and not in a kingdom of man.

Holy Week builds momentum as it approaches Great Friday, which, for Christians, is the most solemn and poignant day of the year. It is the definitive moment of Jesus's Passion and agape. Even on the Cross, he has agape for those who are killing him crying, "Father, forgive them; for they know not what they do" (Luke 23:34). He was killed like a guilty criminal, but the Cross is a symbol of victory. Our reasoning minds tell us the way Jesus died is a curse and a disgrace; however, over two billion people wear the Cross around their necks with pride because Jesus was killed on the Cross for us because of his agape for us. Easter may be the most sublime and reverent day of the year because it is a day of hope and promise that there is eternal life with God in Heaven and that one day our bodies will resurrect. However, we love Jesus not for what he can give us, but because of his incomprehensible agape for us. His self-sacrificial death defines agape and he is worthy of adoration and adulation. The Cross is a sign of victory because on it, Jesus completed his mission for our salvation. Not even death could stop Jesus from fulfilling his mission. In fact, death made it possible. Dying for us is why he came into the world.

Only through Jesus's suffering can we understand his kingship. As Prophet Isaiah prophesied for God,

> I [God] will divide him a portion with the great,
>> and he shall divide the spoil with the strong;
> because he poured out his soul to death,
>> and was numbered with the transgressors
> (Isaiah 53:12).

> Behold, my servant [God's servant] shall prosper,
>> he shall be exalted and lifted up,
>> and shall be very high.
> 14 As many were astonished at him[b]—

his appearance was so marred, beyond
human semblance,
  and his form beyond that of the sons of
men—
15 so shall he startle[c] many nations;
  kings shall shut their mouths because of
him;
for that which has not been told them they
shall see,
  and that which they have not heard they
shall understand (Isaiah 52:13).

This world's kings may be baffled by Jesus - Isaiah's
prophesied Suffering Servant of God - and his
resurrection and the miracles worked in his name by
the Holy Spirit, but for Christians, they are as real as
Heaven.

Jesus knew what he was getting into and the
suffering that was ahead of him. This makes his
agape more compelling than if he did not know
because most people, if they knew, would have run.
As Prophet Isaiah prophesied,

He was oppressed, and he was afflicted,
  yet he opened not his mouth;
like a lamb that is led to the slaughter,
  and like a sheep that before its shearers is
dumb,
  so he opened not his mouth (Isaiah 53:7).

There are a few times when the Gospels say that Jesus prophesied his own death and how it would happen. For example, Jesus told his disciples,

"Behold, we are going up to Jerusalem, and everything that is written of the Son of man by the prophets will be accomplished. 32 For he will be delivered to the Gentiles, and will be mocked and shamefully treated and spit upon; 33 they will scourge him and kill him, and on the third day he will rise" (Luke 18:31b).

Even in agony, Jesus's faith in God his Father remained steadfast. In Gethsemane in anticipation of his "cup" of suffering and death, he "prayed more earnestly; and his sweat became like great drops of blood falling down upon the ground" (Luke 22:44). To God, he prayed, "Abba, Father, all things are possible to thee; remove this cup from me; yet not what I will, but what thou wilt" (Mark 14:36). He was obedient to God's will and submitted to God's power. He was God's perfect servant and a son who adored his Father.

When Jesus was questioned about who he was, even if it meant suffering, he fearlessly told the truth:

The high priest then questioned Jesus about his disciples and his teaching. 20 Jesus answered him, "I have spoken openly to the world; I have always taught in synagogues and in the temple, where all Jews come together; I have said nothing secretly. 21 Why do you ask me? Ask those who have heard me, what I said to them; they know what I said." 22 When he had said this, one of the officers standing by struck Jesus with his hand, saying, "Is that how you answer the high priest?" 23 Jesus answered him, "If I have spoken wrongly, bear witness to the wrong; but if I have spoken rightly, why do you strike me?" (John 18:19).

Still further:

Now the chief priests and the whole council sought false testimony against Jesus that they might put him to death, 60 but they found none, though many false witnesses came forward. At last two came forward 61 and said, "This fellow said, 'I am able to destroy the temple of God, and to build it in three days.'" 62 And the high priest stood up and said, "Have you no answer to make? What is it that these men testify against you?" 63 But Jesus was silent. And the high priest said to him, "I adjure you by the living God, tell us if you are the Christ, the Son of God." 64 Jesus said to him, "You have said so. But I tell you, hereafter you will see the Son of man seated at the right hand of Power, and coming on the clouds of heaven." 65 Then the high priest tore his robes, and said, "He has uttered blasphemy. Why do we still need witnesses? You have now heard his blasphemy. 66 What is your judgment?" They answered, "He deserves death." 67 Then they spat in his face, and struck him; and some slapped him, 68 saying, "Prophesy to us, you Christ! Who is it that struck you?" (Matthew 26:59).

Jesus, my King, not only experienced physical pain for us, but was also belittled, mocked and disgraced for us:

Then the soldiers of the governor took Jesus into the praetorium, and they gathered the whole battalion before him. 28 And they stripped him and put a scarlet robe upon him, 29 and plaiting a crown of thorns they put it on his head, and put a reed in his right hand. And kneeling before him they mocked him, saying, "Hail, King of the Jews!" 30 And they spat upon him, and took the reed and struck him on the head. 31 And when they had mocked him, they stripped him of the robe, and put his own clothes on him, and led him away to crucify him (Matthew 27:27).

My King is the Son of the Most High, yet he was
stepped on like dirt. He suffered many things for me.
The soldiers spat on him. How could they spit on my
King? He lowered himself for me. Who am I am? I
am little and he is great. A devoted servant would lay
down his life for his king, but my King laid down his
life for his servants. What have we done to deserve
such grace? How can we repay him? The only way I
know how to repay him is to emulate him. We must
be willing to sacrifice ourselves for him and the
brethren. They treated him less than a human being
when in reality he was God. It makes no sense, but if
you listen to his words, you will see he did it out of
agape. He was disgraced, but that is why I glorify
him.

The climax of Jesus's Passion is his
crucifixion - an incomprehensible suffering where the
sentenced one dies slowly. With his limbs nailed to
and his body hanging from a wood, Jesus cried with a
loud voice, "My God, my God, why hast thou
forsaken me?" (Mark 15:34 and Matthew 27:46). It
would be hard to find greater suffering - suffering so
great that the Son of God is praying for mercy.
However, Jesus never curses God or His authority.
Knowing he was innocent and was sentenced
unjustly to death, Jesus never separates himself from
God. On the Cross, with a loud voice, Jesus cries out,
"'Father, into thy hands I commit my spirit!' And
having said this he breathed his last" (Luke 23:46). It
was finished. Triumph. Jesus accomplished what he

was meant to do. To his very end, he was a messenger of the truth and fulfilled his mission for the forgiveness of our sins, so we can have eternal life.

Jesus is often referred to as the Good Shepherd - a glorious, edifying and sweet title. In the Old Testament, Psalm 23 refers to the Lord as a shepherd:

A Psalm of David.

The Lord is my shepherd, I shall not want;
2   he makes me lie down in green pastures.
He leads me beside still waters;[a]
3   he restores my soul.[b]
He leads me in paths of righteousness[c]
    for his name's sake.
4 Even though I walk through the valley of the shadow of death,[d]
    I fear no evil;
for thou art with me;
    thy rod and thy staff,
    they comfort me.
5 Thou preparest a table before me
    in the presence of my enemies;
thou anointest my head with oil,
    my cup overflows.
6 Surely[e] goodness and mercy[f] shall follow me
    all the days of my life;

and I shall dwell in the house of the Lord
    for ever.

This title is also used in the in the New Testament.
Jesus tells us,

> I am the good shepherd. The good shepherd
> lays down his life for the sheep. 12 He who is
> a hireling and not a shepherd, whose own the
> sheep are not, sees the wolf coming and leaves
> the sheep and flees; and the wolf snatches
> them and scatters them. 13 He flees because
> he is a hireling and cares nothing for the
> sheep. 14 I am the good shepherd; I know my
> own and my own know me, 15 as the Father
> knows me and I know the Father; and I lay
> down my life for the sheep. 16 And I have
> other sheep, that are not of this fold; I must
> bring them also, and they will heed my voice.
> So there shall be one flock, one shepherd. 17
> For this reason the Father loves me, because I
> lay down my life, that I may take it again. 18
> No one takes it from me, but I lay it down of
> my own accord. I have power to lay it down,
> and I have power to take it again; this charge I
> have received from my Father" (John 10:11).

Jesus is the Good Shepherd because he lay down his
life for us, his flock. He lay down his life everyone,
including those who have not yet heard his voice.

Not one of us unimportant. He is trying to save us all.

Another important Psalm to meditate is Psalm 22, which is often referred to as the Passion Psalm. When you read it, try to hear Jesus's suffering and agony when he prays in Gethsemane and when he is hanging on the Cross. You will see Jesus's humanity as his suffers as a man, but you will also see his confidence in God as God's Son. He has nowhere to go. God is all he has. He trusts in God who gives him strength before he falls apart. Jesus endured to show us we have the power to endure and that we must endure.

In Isaiah, God's Suffering Servant prophecy explains that "he bore the sin of many, and made intercession for the transgressors" (53:12c). We are the transgressors - the sinners in this world - and are far from God, but Jesus interceded for us, so we can have a way to unite with God. Sinful man has no way of entering Heaven and uniting with God on his own. We are unworthy of God because we have rejected Him, as did our parents Adam and Eve, and have no way of making amends with Him. God and His Son Jesus knew this and made a plan to save us from our wicked ways that lead to hell, so we can be with God forever in Heaven. The plan was for perfect Jesus to die for us. He was the only worthy sacrifice to God to redeem sinful man. It hurts God and Jesus for Jesus to be tortured and killed, but they did so willingly to retain justice in a God centered universe.

God's Justice required punishment for sin and Jesus took our place.

> Surely he has borne our griefs[d]
>   and carried our sorrows;[e]
> yet we esteemed him stricken,
>   smitten by God, and afflicted.
> 5 But he was wounded for our transgressions,
>   he was bruised for our iniquities;
> upon him was the chastisement that made us whole,
>   and with his stripes we are healed (Isaiah 53:4).

Only perfect Jesus was a satisfactory substitution for humankind. "The LORD has laid on him the iniquity of us all" (Isaiah 53:6). He satisfied the debt due to God for human sin. "He makes himself an offering for sin" (Isaiah 53:10). His blood was "poured out for many for the forgiveness of sins" (Matthew 26:28). We dishonor God, as did our parents Adam and Eve, with our sin of disobedience. Jesus makes reconciliation possible between God and us. He was perfectly obedient to God's will to the very end of his life. His obedience mends the rift of our disobedience. This is known as atonement, which refers to our redemption and salvation. "By his knowledge shall the righteous one, my servant, make many to be accounted righteous" (Isaiah 53:11). Through Jesus, we are saved and we must accept

Jesus as our Savior to be put right with God. If we do, we will live forever in Paradise with God and Jesus.

I did not fabricate the meaning of agape. The teachings about agape that I have highlighted in this work are the result of studying about, praying to and following Jesus. I humble myself under my Teacher and Master Jesus the Christ who is "the only-begotten Son of God, begotten of the Father before all ages, Light of Light, true God of true God, begotten, not made, of one essence with the Father, by whom all things were made" (The Creed). Unlike Jesus, we are not begotten children of God. We are made by God and if we are true to ourselves, we understand that we are made by Jesus the Christ, who is true God of true God. We who have learned from, worship and abide in Christ are made by him. For, "it is no longer I who live, but Christ who lives in me" (Galatians 2:20).

This work is meant to be a painting in words of the means to union with God. This way people can see the big picture, so there is no longer fear - only hope, comfort and peace - about eternity. The 3000 year old thriving Hindu theology of Brahman, Atman and Moksha is the image and Jesus is the way. I have not focused on Jesus's miracles or resurrection to illustrate his unique position as God's only begotten Son who makes eternal life possible. I have focused on his agape, which if embraced and emulated, will unite one with God who is Agape. Implicit in the theology is the Holy Spirit who, too, is Agape.

TREATISE THREE

THE MESSIAH JESUS

JAMES THOMAS ANGELIDIS

"Hosanna! Blessed is he who comes in the name of
the Lord! Blessed is the kingdom of our father David
that is coming! Hosanna in the highest!"
(Mark 11:9b).

INTRODUCTION

The title Messiah comes from the Hebrew
word "mashiach," which means "anointed one." In
Jewish tradition, it was used to refer to priests and
kings who were anointed with holy oil to consecrate
their positions and signify God's blessing. However,
in the Jewish theology about the end of days, it has
greater significance because it refers to the Messiah
who will usher in God's Kingdom. The Greek term
for the title Messiah is Christ. Jesus's followers
identify Jesus as the Christ. They are known as
Christians. In the following treatise, I will display
Old Testament passages about the Messiah and God's
Kingdom of Heaven and how Jesus makes the
prophecies reality. My goal is to strengthen my
fellow Christians' faith and show Jews that Jesus is
the One.

Some people deny Jesus even existed. But,
the indisputable truth that Jesus was not a fictional
character is that he had disciples who died for him.
Even when tortured, these men never let go. They
had a single mind with the same mission to travel the

world preaching the good news of Jesus. They were peaceful martyrs and their devotion to Jesus cannot be denied. To those who do not believe in Jesus's disciples, it is because of the hardness of their hearts. One must have to work hard to not believe in them. To reject their conviction, acts, martyrdoms and existences is pure madness.

Jesus was a Jew of the highest level. He knew the Hebrew Scriptures inside and out, from beginning to end. He knew the Hebrew Scriptures so well that he could quote them. Some people may question if what is ascribed to Jesus in the Gospels are his authentic words. The words may or may not be verbatim, but I have no doubt that the words are a reflection of his words. The Gospel of Mark is estimated to be written about 30-35 years after Jesus was crucified, only a generation after Jesus lived. Why is it harder to believe that the words ascribed to Jesus are based on his own words than are words fabricated by the Gospel writers? Said differently, why is it easier to believe that the words are the Gospel writers' words and not based on Jesus's words?

Jewish sage and scholar Hillel the Elder was born about 100 years before Jesus. He is quoted saying, "That which is hateful to you, do not do to your neighbor. That is the whole Torah; the rest is commentary. Go and study it." As an erudite Jew, Jesus knew of Hillel and his teachings. However, Jesus revolutionized Hillel's worldly proverb and made it divine by replacing hate with love. Jesus says, "So whatever you wish that men would do to you, do so to them; for this is the law and the prophets" (Matthew 7:12). Elsewhere, Jesus says, "You shall love your neighbor as yourself" (Matthew 22:39).

Jesus applied Old Testament imagery to his teachings and also used it to illustrate his role as the Messiah. In the Old Testament, Israel is described as God's Vine:

> Psalm 80:8 (RSV)
> Prayer for Israel's Restoration
> To the choirmaster: according to Lilies. A Testimony of Asaph. A Psalm.
> 8 Thou didst bring a vine out of Egypt [when the Jews were slaves];
>   thou didst drive out the nations and plant it.
> 9 Thou didst clear the ground for it;
>   it took deep root and filled the land.
> 10 The mountains were covered with its shade,
>   the mighty cedars with its branches;
> 11 it sent out its branches to the sea,
>   and its shoots to the River.
> 12 Why then hast thou broken down its walls,
>   so that all who pass along the way pluck its fruit?
> 13 The boar from the forest ravages it,
>   and all that move in the field feed on it.

14 Turn again, O God of hosts!
  Look down from heaven, and see;
have regard for this vine,
15   the stock which thy right hand
planted.[b]
16 They have burned it with fire, they have
cut it down;
  may they perish at the rebuke of thy
countenance!
17 But let thy hand be upon the man of thy
right hand,
  the son of man whom thou hast made strong
for thyself!
18 Then we will never turn back from thee;
  give us life, and we will call on thy name!
19 Restore us, O LORD God of hosts!
  let thy face shine, that we may be saved!

Jesus identifies himself as the above son of man who sits at the right hand of God. He calls himself the True Vine with his faithful as the branches that bear fruit and that God is the Vinedresser:

John 15:1 (RSV)
Jesus the True Vine
15 "I am the true vine, and my Father is the vinedresser. 2 Every branch of mine that bears no fruit, he takes away, and every branch that does bear fruit he prunes, that it may bear more fruit. 3 You are already made clean by

the word which I have spoken to you. 4 Abide in me, and I in you. As the branch cannot bear fruit by itself, unless it abides in the vine, neither can you, unless you abide in me. 5 I am the vine, you are the branches. He who abides in me, and I in him, he it is that bears much fruit, for apart from me you can do nothing. 6 If a man does not abide in me, he is cast forth as a branch and withers; and the branches are gathered, thrown into the fire and burned. 7 If you abide in me, and my words abide in you, ask whatever you will, and it shall be done for you. 8 By this my Father is glorified, that you bear much fruit, and so prove to be my disciples. 9 As the Father has loved me, so have I loved you; abide in my love. 10 If you keep my commandments, you will abide in my love, just as I have kept my Father's commandments and abide in his love. 11 These things I have spoken to you, that my joy may be in you, and that your joy may be full. 12 "This is my commandment, that you love one another as I have loved you.13 Greater love has no man than this, that a man lay down his life for his friends. 14 You are my friends if you do what I command you. 15 No longer do I call you servants,[a] for the servant[b] does not know what his master is doing; but I have called you friends, for all that I have heard from my Father I have made known to you. 16 You did not choose me, but I chose you and appointed you that you should go and bear fruit and that your fruit should abide; so that whatever you ask the Father in my name, he may give it to you. 17 This I command you, to love one another.

Similarly, Jesus was aware of the Old Testament imagery of God as Shepherd who tends to His people, His flock:

Ezekiel 34:1 (RSV)
Israel's False Shepherds
34 The word of the LORD came to me: 2 "Son of man, prophesy against the shepherds of Israel, prophesy, and say to them, even to the shepherds, Thus says the Lord GOD: Ho, shepherds of Israel who have been feeding yourselves! Should not shepherds feed the sheep? 3 You eat the fat, you clothe yourselves with the wool, you slaughter the fatlings; but you do not feed the sheep. 4 The weak you have not strengthened, the sick you have not healed, the crippled you have not bound up, the strayed you have not brought back, the lost you have not sought, and with force and harshness you have ruled them. 5 So they were scattered, because there was no shepherd; and they became food for all the wild beasts. 6 My sheep were scattered, they

wandered over all the mountains and on every high hill; my sheep were scattered over all the face of the earth, with none to search or seek for them.

7 "Therefore, you shepherds, hear the word of the LORD: 8 As I live, says the Lord GOD, because my sheep have become a prey, and my sheep have become food for all the wild beasts, since there was no shepherd; and because my shepherds have not searched for my sheep, but the shepherds have fed themselves, and have not fed my sheep; 9 therefore, you shepherds, hear the word of the LORD: 10 Thus says the Lord GOD, Behold, I am against the shepherds; and I will require my sheep at their hand, and put a stop to their feeding the sheep; no longer shall the shepherds feed themselves. I will rescue my sheep from their mouths, that they may not be food for them.

God, the True Shepherd
11 "For thus says the Lord GOD: Behold, I, I myself will search for my sheep, and will seek them out. 12 As a shepherd seeks out his flock when some of his sheep[a] have been scattered abroad, so will I seek out my sheep; and I will rescue them from all places where they have been scattered on a day of clouds and thick darkness. 13 And I will bring them

out from the peoples, and gather them from the countries, and will bring them into their own land; and I will feed them on the mountains of Israel, by the fountains, and in all the inhabited places of the country. 14 I will feed them with good pasture, and upon the mountain heights of Israel shall be their pasture; there they shall lie down in good grazing land, and on fat pasture they shall feed on the mountains of Israel. 15 I myself will be the shepherd of my sheep, and I will make them lie down, says the Lord GOD. 16 I will seek the lost, and I will bring back the strayed, and I will bind up the crippled, and I will strengthen the weak, and the fat and the strong I will watch over;[b] I will feed them in justice. 17 "As for you, my flock, thus says the Lord GOD: Behold, I judge between sheep and sheep, rams and he-goats. 18 Is it not enough for you to feed on the good pasture, that you must tread down with your feet the rest of your pasture; and to drink of clear water, that you must foul the rest with your feet? 19 And must my sheep eat what you have trodden with your feet, and drink what you have fouled with your feet? 20 "Therefore, thus says the Lord GOD to them: Behold, I, I myself will judge between the fat sheep and the lean sheep. 21 Because you push with side and shoulder, and thrust at all the weak with your horns, till you have scattered them abroad, 22 I will save my flock, they shall no longer be a prey; and I will judge between sheep and sheep. 23 And I will set up over them one shepherd, my servant David, and he shall feed them: he shall feed them and be their shepherd. 24 And I, the LORD, will be their God, and my servant David shall be prince among them; I, the LORD, have spoken. 25 "I will make with them a covenant of peace and banish wild beasts from the land, so that they may dwell securely in the wilderness and sleep in the woods.26 And I will make them and the places round about my hill a blessing; and I will send down the showers in their season; they shall be showers of blessing.27 And the trees of the field shall yield their fruit, and the earth shall yield its increase, and they shall be secure in their land; and they shall know that I am the LORD, when I break the bars of their yoke, and deliver them from the hand of those who enslaved them. 28 They shall no more be a prey to the nations, nor shall the beasts of the land devour them; they shall dwell securely, and none shall make them afraid. 29 And I will provide for them prosperous[c] plantations so that they shall no more be consumed with hunger in the land, and no longer suffer the reproach of the nations. 30

And they shall know that I, the LORD their God, am with them, and that they, the house of Israel, are my people, says the Lord GOD. 31 And you are my sheep, the sheep of my pasture,[d] and I am your God, says the Lord GOD."

As Jesus does with the Old Testament vine imagery, he uses the shepherd imagery to describe himself. He takes the shepherd imagery a step further and declares that he is the Good Shepherd who lays down his life for God's flock:

John 10:1 (RSV)
Jesus the Good Shepherd
10 "Truly, truly, I say to you, he who does not enter the sheepfold by the door but climbs in by another way, that man is a thief and a robber; 2 but he who enters by the door is the shepherd of the sheep. 3 To him the gatekeeper opens; the sheep hear his voice, and he calls his own sheep by name and leads them out. 4 When he has brought out all his own, he goes before them, and the sheep follow him, for they know his voice. 5 A stranger they will not follow, but they will flee from him, for they do not know the voice of strangers." 6 This figure Jesus used with them, but they did not understand what he was saying to them. 7 So Jesus again said to them,

"Truly, truly, I say to you, I am the door of the sheep. 8 All who came before me are thieves and robbers; but the sheep did not heed them. 9 I am the door; if any one enters by me, he will be saved, and will go in and out and find pasture. 10 The thief comes only to steal and kill and destroy; I came that they may have life, and have it abundantly. 11 I am the good shepherd. The good shepherd lays down his life for the sheep. 12 He who is a hireling and not a shepherd, whose own the sheep are not, sees the wolf coming and leaves the sheep and flees; and the wolf snatches them and scatters them. 13 He flees because he is a hireling and cares nothing for the sheep. 14 I am the good shepherd; I know my own and my own know me, 15 as the Father knows me and I know the Father; and I lay down my life for the sheep. 16 And I have other sheep, that are not of this fold; I must bring them also, and they will heed my voice. So there shall be one flock, one shepherd. 17 For this reason the Father loves me, because I lay down my life, that I may take it again. 18 No one takes it from me, but I lay it down of my own accord. I have power to lay it down, and I have power to take it again; this charge I have received from my Father."

JESUS

Below are the Old Testament prophecies that specify Jesus as the Messiah.

Isaiah 7:10 (RSV)
Isaiah Gives Ahaz the Sign of Immanuel
10 Again the LORD spoke to Ahaz, 11 "Ask a sign of the LORD your God; let it be deep as Sheol or high as heaven." 12 But Ahaz said, "I will not ask, and I will not put the LORD to the test." 13 And he said, "Hear then, O house of David! Is it too little for you to weary men, that you weary my God also? 14 Therefore the Lord himself will give you a sign. Behold, a young woman [or virgin] shall conceive and bear[c] a son, and shall call his name Imman'u-el [meaning, God is with us] 15 He shall eat curds and honey when he knows how to refuse the evil and choose the good. 16 For before the child knows how to refuse the evil and choose the good, the land before whose two kings you are in dread will be deserted. 17 The LORD will bring upon you and upon your people and upon your father's house such days as have not come since the day that E'phraim departed from Judah—the king of Assyria."

As we learn in Matthew and Luke, the Virgin Mother Mary gave birth to Jesus, who is God.

> Micah 5:2 (RSV)
> The Ruler from Bethlehem
> 2 [c] But you, O Bethlehem Eph'rathah,
>   who are little to be among the clans of Judah,
> from you shall come forth for me
>   one who is to be ruler in Israel,
> whose origin is from of old,
>   from ancient days.
> 3 Therefore he shall give them up until the time
>   when she who is in travail has brought forth;
> then the rest of his brethren shall return
>   to the people of Israel.
> 4 And he shall stand and feed his flock in the strength of the LORD,
>   in the majesty of the name of the LORD his God.
> And they shall dwell secure, for now he shall be great
>   to the ends of the earth.

As we learn in Matthew, Jesus was born in Bethlehem.

> Isaiah 61:1 (RSV)
> The Good News of Deliverance

61 The Spirit of the Lord GOD is upon me,
   because the LORD has anointed me
to bring good tidings to the afflicted;[a]
   he has sent me to bind up the brokenhearted,
to proclaim liberty to the captives,
   and the opening of the prison[b] to those
who are bound;
2 to proclaim the year of the LORD's favor,
   and the day of vengeance of our God;
   to comfort all who mourn;
3 to grant to those who mourn in Zion—
   to give them a garland instead of ashes,
the oil of gladness instead of mourning,
   the mantle of praise instead of a faint spirit;
that they may be called oaks of righteousness,
   the planting of the LORD, that he may be
glorified.

*As we learn in Luke, Jesus recites part of this passage
in a Nazarene synagogue on the Sabbath day
announcing to the congregation that he is the
Messiah.*

Zechariah 9:9 (RSV)
The Coming Ruler of God's People
9 Rejoice greatly, O daughter of Zion!
   Shout aloud, O daughter of Jerusalem!
Lo, your king comes to you;
   triumphant and victorious is he,
humble and riding on an ass,

on a colt the foal of an ass.
10 I will cut off the chariot from E'phraim
   and the war horse from Jerusalem;
and the battle bow shall be cut off,
   and he shall command peace to the nations;
his dominion shall be from sea to sea,
   and from the River to the ends of the earth.

As we learn in Matthew, during Palm Sunday, Jesus is greeted by the crowds as their king, humble and riding on an ass.

Isaiah 9:1 (RSV)
The Righteous Reign of the Coming King
9 [a] But there will be no gloom for her that was in anguish. In the former time he brought into contempt the land of Zeb'ulun and the land of Naph'tali, but in the latter time he will make glorious the way of the sea, the land beyond the Jordan, Galilee of the nations.
2 [b] The people who walked in darkness
   have seen a great light;
those who dwelt in a land of deep darkness,
   on them has light shined.
3 Thou hast multiplied the nation,
   thou hast increased its joy;
they rejoice before thee
   as with joy at the harvest,
   as men rejoice when they divide the spoil.
4 For the yoke of his burden,

and the staff for his shoulder,
 the rod of his oppressor,
 thou hast broken as on the day of Mid'ian.
5 For every boot of the tramping warrior in battle tumult
 and every garment rolled in blood
 will be burned as fuel for the fire.
6 For to us a child is born,
 to us a son is given;
and the government will be upon his shoulder,
 and his name will be called
"Wonderful Counselor, Mighty God,
 Everlasting Father, Prince of Peace."
7 Of the increase of his government and of peace
 there will be no end,
upon the throne of David, and over his kingdom,
 to establish it, and to uphold it
with justice and with righteousness
 from this time forth and for evermore.
The zeal of the LORD of hosts will do this.

Jesus is none other than the Wonderful Counselor, Mighty God, Everlasting Father, Prince of Peace.

Psalm 72:1 (RSV)
Prayer for Guidance and Support for the King
A Psalm of Solomon.
72 Give the king thy justice, O God,

and thy righteousness to the royal son!

2 May he judge thy people with righteousness,
    and thy poor with justice!

3 Let the mountains bear prosperity for the
people,
    and the hills, in righteousness!

4 May he defend the cause of the poor of the
people,
    give deliverance to the needy,
    and crush the oppressor!

5 May he live[a] while the sun endures,
    and as long as the moon, throughout all
generations!

6 May he be like rain that falls on the mown
grass,
    like showers that water the earth!

7 In his days may righteousness flourish,
    and peace abound, till the moon be no more!

8 May he have dominion from sea to sea,
    and from the River to the ends of the earth!

9 May his foes[b] bow down before him,
    and his enemies lick the dust!

10 May the kings of Tarshish and of the isles
    render him tribute,
may the kings of Sheba and Seba bring gifts!

11 May all kings fall down before him,
    all nations serve him!

12 For he delivers the needy when he calls,
    the poor and him who has no helper.

13 He has pity on the weak and the needy,

and saves the lives of the needy.

14 From oppression and violence he redeems
their life;

and precious is their blood in his sight.

Jesus is the Messiah King.

Isaiah 11:1 (RSV)

The Peaceful Kingdom

11 There shall come forth a shoot from the
stump of Jesse,

and a branch shall grow out of his roots.

2 And the Spirit of the LORD shall rest upon
him,

the spirit of wisdom and understanding,

the spirit of counsel and might,

the spirit of knowledge and the fear of the
LORD.

3 And his delight shall be in the fear of the
LORD.

He shall not judge by what his eyes see,

or decide by what his ears hear;

4 but with righteousness he shall judge the
poor,

and decide with equity for the meek of the
earth;

and he shall smite the earth with the rod of his
mouth,

and with the breath of his lips he shall slay
the wicked.

5 Righteousness shall be the girdle of his
waist,

and faithfulness the girdle of his loins.

Again, Jesus fulfills the role as the Messiah King.

Psalm 22:1 (RSV)
Plea for Deliverance from Suffering and
Hostility
To the choirmaster: according to The Hind of
the Dawn. A Psalm of David.
22 My God, my God, why hast thou forsaken
me?

Why art thou so far from helping me, from
the words of my groaning?
2 O my God, I cry by day, but thou dost not
answer;

and by night, but find no rest.
3 Yet thou art holy,

enthroned on the praises of Israel.
4 In thee our fathers trusted;

they trusted, and thou didst deliver them.
5 To thee they cried, and were saved;

in thee they trusted, and were not
disappointed.
6 But I am a worm, and no man;

scorned by men, and despised by the people.
7 All who see me mock at me,

they make mouths at me, they wag their
heads;

8 "He committed his cause to the LORD; let him deliver him,

   let him rescue him, for he delights in him!"

9 Yet thou art he who took me from the womb;

   thou didst keep me safe upon my mother's breasts.

10 Upon thee was I cast from my birth,

   and since my mother bore me thou hast been my God.

11 Be not far from me,

   for trouble is near

   and there is none to help.

12 Many bulls encompass me,

   strong bulls of Bashan surround me;

13 they open wide their mouths at me,

   like a ravening and roaring lion.

14 I am poured out like water,

   and all my bones are out of joint;

my heart is like wax,

   it is melted within my breast;

15 my strength is dried up like a potsherd,

   and my tongue cleaves to my jaws;

   thou dost lay me in the dust of death.

16 Yea, dogs are round about me;

   a company of evildoers encircle me;

   they have pierced[a] my hands and feet—

17 I can count all my bones—

   they stare and gloat over me;

18 they divide my garments among them,

and for my raiment they cast lots.

19 But thou, O LORD, be not far off!

O thou my help, hasten to my aid!

20 Deliver my soul from the sword,

my life[b] from the power of the dog!

21 Save me from the mouth of the lion,

my afflicted soul[c] from the horns of the wild oxen!

22 I will tell of thy name to my brethren;

in the midst of the congregation I will praise thee:

23 You who fear the LORD, praise him!

all you sons of Jacob, glorify him,

and stand in awe of him, all you sons of Israel!

24 For he has not despised or abhorred

the affliction of the afflicted;

and he has not hid his face from him,

but has heard, when he cried to him.

25 From thee comes my praise in the great congregation;

my vows I will pay before those who fear him.

26 The afflicted[d] shall eat and be satisfied;

those who seek him shall praise the LORD!

May your hearts live for ever!

27 All the ends of the earth shall remember

and turn to the LORD;

and all the families of the nations

shall worship before him.[e]

28 For dominion belongs to the LORD,
   and he rules over the nations.
29 Yea, to him[f] shall all the proud of the
earth bow down;
   before him shall bow all who go down to the
dust,
   and he who cannot keep himself alive.
30 Posterity shall serve him;
   men shall tell of the Lord to the coming
generation,
31 and proclaim his deliverance to a people
yet unborn,
   that he has wrought it.

*As we learn in Matthew, Jesus quotes part of this
Psalm when he is dying on the Cross.*

GOD'S SERVANT

*The Jewish nation sees itself as God's Chosen
Servant. During moments of ecstasy and affliction it
is obedient to God's will. It never questions God's
plan and accepts its fate. On the Cross, Jesus
represents the nobility and affliction of the Jewish
nation. He becomes God's Chosen Servant. He is the
perfect Jew and represents everything a Jew should
be. Below are two passages from Isaiah that talk
about God's Chosen Servant. In them, the Jewish
nation sees itself and Christians see Jesus.*

Isaiah 42:1 (RSV)

The Servant, a Light to the Nations

42 Behold my servant, whom I uphold,
  my chosen, in whom my soul delights;
I have put my Spirit upon him,
  he will bring forth justice to the nations.
2 He will not cry or lift up his voice,
  or make it heard in the street;
3 a bruised reed he will not break,
  and a dimly burning wick he will not
quench;
  he will faithfully bring forth justice.
4 He will not fail[a] or be discouraged[b]
  till he has established justice in the earth;
  and the coastlands wait for his law.

Isaiah 52:13-53:12 (RSV)

The Suffering Servant

13 Behold, my servant shall prosper,
  he shall be exalted and lifted up,
  and shall be very high.
14 As many were astonished at him[b]—
  his appearance was so marred, beyond
human semblance,
  and his form beyond that of the sons of
men—
15 so shall he startle[c] many nations;
  kings shall shut their mouths because of
him;

for that which has not been told them they shall see,

and that which they have not heard they shall understand.

53 Who has believed what we have heard?

And to whom has the arm of the LORD been revealed?

2 For he grew up before him like a young plant,

and like a root out of dry ground;

he had no form or comeliness that we should look at him,

and no beauty that we should desire him.

3 He was despised and rejected[d] by men;

a man of sorrows,[e] and acquainted with grief;[f]

and as one from whom men hide their faces

he was despised, and we esteemed him not.

4 Surely he has borne our griefs[g]

and carried our sorrows;[h]

yet we esteemed him stricken,

smitten by God, and afflicted.

5 But he was wounded for our transgressions,

he was bruised for our iniquities;

upon him was the chastisement that made us whole,

and with his stripes we are healed.

6 All we like sheep have gone astray;

we have turned every one to his own way;

and the Lord has laid on him
    the iniquity of us all.
7 He was oppressed, and he was afflicted,
    yet he opened not his mouth;
like a lamb that is led to the slaughter,
    and like a sheep that before its shearers is
dumb,
    so he opened not his mouth.
8 By oppression and judgment he was taken
away;
    and as for his generation, who considered
that he was cut off out of the land of the
living,
    stricken for the transgression of my people?
9 And they made his grave with the wicked
    and with a rich man in his death,
although he had done no violence,
    and there was no deceit in his mouth.
10 Yet it was the will of the Lord to bruise
him;
    he has put him to grief;[i]
when he makes himself[j] an offering for sin,
    he shall see his offspring, he shall prolong
his days;
the will of the Lord shall prosper in his hand;
11   he shall see the fruit of the travail of his
soul and be satisfied;
by his knowledge shall the righteous one, my
servant,
    make many to be accounted righteous;

and he shall bear their iniquities.
12 Therefore I will divide him a portion with the great,
  and he shall divide the spoil with the strong;
because he poured out his soul to death,
  and was numbered with the transgressors;
yet he bore the sin of many,
  and made intercession for the transgressors.

As the Messiah, Jesus is the embodiment of Israel. He is Israel personified. He is the culmination of Israel, its fulfillment and everything it was meant to be.

A NEW COVENANT OF THE HEART

Jeremiah 31:31 (RSV)
A New Covenant
31 "Behold, the days are coming, says the LORD, when I will make a new covenant with the house of Israel and the house of Judah, 32 not like the covenant which I made with their fathers when I took them by the hand to bring them out of the land of Egypt, my covenant which they broke, though I was their husband, says the LORD. 33 But this is the covenant which I will make with the house of Israel after those days, says the LORD: I will put my law within them, and I will write it upon their

hearts; and I will be their God, and they shall be my people. 34 And no longer shall each man teach his neighbor and each his brother, saying, 'Know the LORD,' for they shall all know me, from the least of them to the greatest, says the LORD; for I will forgive their iniquity, and I will remember their sin no more."

Jesus gave us this new covenant written upon our hearts. He fulfilled this promise and taught us with his words and showed us with his death the meaning of love. The two great commandments are to "love the Lord your God with all your heart, and with all your soul, and with all your mind" and to "love your neighbor as yourself. On these two commandments depend all the law and the prophets" (Matthew 22.36) and they cannot be practiced unless they are written upon one's heart.

JESUS'S RESURRECTION

After Jesus's crucifixion and death, Jesus's body was laid in a new rock tomb secured by a great stone. On the third day, when the women visited the tomb, they did not find his body. Then, he appeared to them and his disciples breathing, speaking, walking and even eating in flesh and bones. His resurrection was prophesied in the Old Testament. So, too, was his role as our Savior from Death.

In Psalm 16:8 (RSV), King David prophesied,

8 I keep the Lord always before me;
   because he is at my right hand, I shall not
be moved.
9 Therefore my heart is glad, and my soul
rejoices;
   my body also dwells secure.
10 For thou dost not give me up to Sheol,
   or let thy godly one see the Pit.
11 Thou dost show me the path of life;
   in thy presence there is fulness of joy,
   in thy right hand are pleasures for
evermore.

In Job 19:25 (RSV), Job declares,

25 For I know that my Redeemer[b] lives,
   and at last he will stand upon the earth;[c]
26 and after my skin has been thus destroyed,
   then from[d] my flesh I shall see God,[e]
27 whom I shall see on my side,[f]
   and my eyes shall behold, and not another.

In the television news documentary The Search for Jesus (2000), Peter Jennings reports his findings on Jesus, including the historical integrity of Jesus's Resurrection.

Meyer: "One of the things I believe that early Christians did is they took the model of the mystery religions, they took that story and retold that story as the story of Jesus."

Jennings: "But the mystery religions and their gods lost all credibility centuries ago. Not so with the resurrection of Jesus. His followers stuck to their story even though they were persecuted. And, as we know the Jesus movement grew and flourished. Which is why some eminent scholars believe there was indeed a resurrection."

Wright: "I simply cannot explain why Christianity began without it. I have already said, there were many other messianic or would be messianic movements around in the first century. Routinely, they ended with the violent death of the founder. After that, what happens? The followers either all get killed, as well, or if they are any of them left, they have a choice: they either quite the revolution or they find themselves another messiah. We have example of people doing both. If Jesus had died and stayed dead, they would either have given up the movement or they would have found another messiah. Something extraordinary happened which convinced them that Jesus was the Messiah."

Jennings: "And, over 300 hundred years after Jesus's execution, Christianity was the official religion of the Roman Empire. 2000 years later, Christians from all over the world venerate the place in Jerusalem where it is said Jesus rose from his tomb."

Fredriksen: "I know in their own terms what they saw was the raised Jesus. That's what they say and that all the historic evidence we have afterwards attests to their conviction that that's what they saw. I'm not saying that they really did see the raised Jesus. I wasn't there. I don't know what they saw, but I do know, as a historian, that they must have seen something."

Jennings: "And, even the most skeptical of scholars and historians agree on this: In his brief life, Jesus of Nazareth probably met and spoke with no more than a few thousand people. He wrote nothing. He commanded no great army. And, he spent most of his time with the poor and the outcast. But, he had a vision for a just world, which was so vivid and which moved him so powerfully that he was willing to die for it. And, after his death, his

vision somehow transformed the world.
Miraculous."

*- Peter Jennings, Anchor of ABC's World
News Tonight.*
*- Marvin Meyer, Author "Magic and Ritual in
the Ancient World."*
*- Reverend N.T. Wright, Canon Theologian of
Westminster Abbey.*
- Paula Fredriksen, Boston University.

MESSIANIC WINE IN GOD'S KINGDOM OF HEAVEN

*If Jesus can rise from the dead, he can also perform
signs revealing his divinity. If he can resurrect from
the dead, he can transform the natural rhythm of the
cosmos. Through the Messiah's blood, the natural
rhythm of the cosmos no longer behaves like water
and takes on qualities of wine. Jesus performed many
signs revealing his divinity that are irrational, but
they all point to the glory of God. They are not
imaginary. They are as real as God's Kingdom of
Heaven. Below are the Old Testament passages that
describe God's Kingdom of Heaven, which at the
moment on this earth takes on qualities of wine.*

Isaiah 55:1 (RSV)
An Invitation to Abundant Life

55 "Ho, every one who thirsts,
  come to the waters;
and he who has no money,
  come, buy and eat!
Come, buy wine and milk
  without money and without price.
2 Why do you spend your money for that
which is not bread,
  and your labor for that which does not
satisfy?
Hearken diligently to me, and eat what is
good,
  and delight yourselves in fatness.
3 Incline your ear, and come to me;
  hear, that your soul may live;
and I will make with you an everlasting
covenant,
  my steadfast, sure love for David.
4 Behold, I made him a witness to the peoples,
  a leader and commander for the peoples.
5 Behold, you shall call nations that you know
not,
  and nations that knew you not shall run to
you,
because of the LORD your God, and of the
Holy One of Israel,
  for he has glorified you.
6 "Seek the LORD while he may be found,
  call upon him while he is near;
7 let the wicked forsake his way,

and the unrighteous man his thoughts;
let him return to the LORD, that he may have
mercy on him,
    and to our God, for he will abundantly
pardon.
8 For my thoughts are not your thoughts,
    neither are your ways my ways, says the
LORD.
9 For as the heavens are higher than the earth,
    so are my ways higher than your ways
    and my thoughts than your thoughts.
10 "For as the rain and the snow come down
from heaven,
    and return not thither but water the earth,
making it bring forth and sprout,
    giving seed to the sower and bread to the
eater,
11 so shall my word be that goes forth from
my mouth;
    it shall not return to me empty,
but it shall accomplish that which I purpose,
    and prosper in the thing for which I sent it.
12 "For you shall go out in joy,
    and be led forth in peace;
the mountains and the hills before you
    shall break forth into singing,
    and all the trees of the field shall clap their
hands.
13 Instead of the thorn shall come up the
cypress;

instead of the brier shall come up the myrtle;
and it shall be to the LORD for a memorial,

for an everlasting sign which shall not be cut
off."

Jeremiah 31:7 (RSV)

The Joyful Return of the Exiles

7 For thus says the LORD:

"Sing aloud with gladness for Jacob,

and raise shouts for the chief of the nations;
proclaim, give praise, and say,

'The LORD has saved his people,

the remnant of Israel.'

8 Behold, I will bring them from the north
country,

and gather them from the farthest parts of
the earth,

among them the blind and the lame,

the woman with child and her who is in
travail, together;

a great company, they shall return here.

9 With weeping they shall come,

and with consolations[e] I will lead them
back,

I will make them walk by brooks of water,

in a straight path in which they shall not
stumble;

for I am a father to Israel,

and E'phraim is my first-born.

10 "Hear the word of the LORD, O nations,

and declare it in the coastlands afar off;
say, 'He who scattered Israel will gather him,
  and will keep him as a shepherd keeps his
flock.'
11 For the LORD has ransomed Jacob,
  and has redeemed him from hands too
strong for him.
12 They shall come and sing aloud on the
height of Zion,
  and they shall be radiant over the goodness
of the LORD,
over the grain, the wine, and the oil,
  and over the young of the flock and the
herd;
their life shall be like a watered garden,
  and they shall languish no more.
13 Then shall the maidens rejoice in the
dance,
  and the young men and the old shall be
merry.
I will turn their mourning into joy,
  I will comfort them, and give them gladness
for sorrow.
14 I will feast the soul of the priests with
abundance,
  and my people shall be satisfied with my
goodness,
          says the LORD."

Micah 4:1 (RSV)

Peace and Security through Obedience

4 It shall come to pass in the latter days
    that the mountain of the house of the LORD
shall be established as the highest of the
mountains,
    and shall be raised up above the hills;
and peoples shall flow to it,
2   and many nations shall come, and say:
"Come, let us go up to the mountain of the
LORD,
    to the house of the God of Jacob;
that he may teach us his ways
    and we may walk in his paths."
For out of Zion shall go forth the law,
    and the word of the LORD from Jerusalem.
3 He shall judge between many peoples,
    and shall decide for strong nations afar off;
and they shall beat their swords into
plowshares,
    and their spears into pruning hooks;
nation shall not lift up sword against nation,
    neither shall they learn war any more;
4 but they shall sit every man under his vine
and under his fig tree,
    and none shall make them afraid;
    for the mouth of the LORD of hosts has
spoken.
5 For all the peoples walk
    each in the name of its god,

but we will walk in the name of the LORD our God
  for ever and ever.

Micah 4:6 (RSV)
Restoration Promised after Exile
6 In that day, says the LORD,
  I will assemble the lame
and gather those who have been driven away,
  and those whom I have afflicted;
7 and the lame I will make the remnant;
  and those who were cast off, a strong nation;
and the LORD will reign over them in Mount Zion
  from this time forth and for evermore.
8 And you, O tower of the flock,
  hill of the daughter of Zion,
to you shall it come,
  the former dominion shall come,
  the kingdom of the daughter of Jerusalem.
9 Now why do you cry aloud?
  Is there no king in you?
Has your counselor perished,
  that pangs have seized you like a woman in travail?
10 Writhe and groan,[a] O daughter of Zion,
  like a woman in travail;
for now you shall go forth from the city
  and dwell in the open country;
  you shall go to Babylon.

There you shall be rescued,
  there the LORD will redeem you
  from the hand of your enemies.
11 Now many nations
  are assembled against you,
saying, "Let her be profaned,
  and let our eyes gaze upon Zion."
12 But they do not know
  the thoughts of the LORD,
they do not understand his plan,
  that he has gathered them as sheaves to the
threshing floor.
13 Arise and thresh,
  O daughter of Zion,
for I will make your horn iron
  and your hoofs bronze;
you shall beat in pieces many peoples,
  and shall[b] devote their gain to the LORD,
  their wealth to the Lord of the whole earth.

Isaiah 25:6 (RSV)
Praise for Deliverance from Oppression
6 On this mountain the LORD of hosts will
make for all peoples a feast of fat things, a
feast of wine on the lees, of fat things full of
marrow, of wine on the lees well refined. 7
And he will destroy on this mountain the
covering that is cast over all peoples, the veil
that is spread over all nations. 8 He will
swallow up death for ever, and the Lord GOD

will wipe away tears from all faces, and the reproach of his people he will take away from all the earth; for the LORD has spoken. 9 It will be said on that day, "Lo, this is our God; we have waited for him, that he might save us. This is the LORD; we have waited for him; let us be glad and rejoice in his salvation."

Amos 9:11 (RSV)
The Restoration of David's Kingdom
11 "In that day I will raise up
   the booth of David that is fallen
and repair its breaches,
   and raise up its ruins,
   and rebuild it as in the days of old;
12 that they may possess the remnant of Edom
   and all the nations who are called by my name,"
   says the LORD who does this.
13 "Behold, the days are coming," says the LORD,
   "when the plowman shall overtake the reaper
   and the treader of grapes him who sows the seed;
the mountains shall drip sweet wine,
   and all the hills shall flow with it.
14 I will restore the fortunes of my people Israel,

and they shall rebuild the ruined cities and inhabit them;
they shall plant vineyards and drink their wine,
    and they shall make gardens and eat their fruit.
15 I will plant them upon their land,
    and they shall never again be plucked up
    out of the land which I have given them,"
            says the LORD your God.

Joel 3:17 (RSV)

The Glorious Future of Judah

17 "So you shall know that I am the LORD your God,
    who dwell in Zion, my holy mountain.
And Jerusalem shall be holy
    and strangers shall never again pass through it.
18 "And in that day
the mountains shall drip sweet wine,
    and the hills shall flow with milk,
and all the stream beds of Judah
    shall flow with water;
and a fountain shall come forth from the house of the LORD
    and water the valley of Shittim.
19 "Egypt shall become a desolation
    and Edom a desolate wilderness,
for the violence done to the people of Judah,

because they have shed innocent blood in
their land.
20 But Judah shall be inhabited for ever,
and Jerusalem to all generations.
21 I will avenge their blood, and I will not
clear the guilty,[c]
for the LORD dwells in Zion."

*God's Kingdom of Heaven has begun. It is here. It is
among us, but it is reserved for those who are faithful
and devoted to Jesus, for those who live by his two
great commandments to "love the Lord your God
with all your heart, and with all your soul, and with
all your mind" and to "love your neighbor as
yourself. On these two commandments depend all the
law and the prophets" (Matthew 22:36).*

JESUS'S SECOND COMING

*If we recognize Jesus as the Messiah and follow and
emulate him, we will be saved from death and enter
God's Kingdom of Heaven and be rewarded with
Resurrection. If we do not, death is our end. At
Jesus's Second Coming, he will be the Righteous
Judge and the living must be able to recognize him,
so, like those in God's Kingdom of Heaven, their
souls and bodies will not perish. Jesus's physical
appearance will not indicate his status; rather, we
will know him by his speech, actions and soul. This is*

*only possible if we read the New Testament. Below
are the Old Testament passages that describe Jesus's
Second Coming.*

Zephaniah 2:1 (RSV)
Judgment on Israel's Enemies
2 Come together and hold assembly,
O shameless nation,
2 before you are driven away
   like the drifting chaff,[a]
before there comes upon you
   the fierce anger of the LORD,
before there comes upon you
   the day of the wrath of the LORD.
3 Seek the LORD, all you humble of the land,
   who do his commands;
seek righteousness, seek humility;
   perhaps you may be hidden
   on the day of the wrath of the LORD.

Isaiah 27:1 (RSV)
Israel's Redemption
27 In that day the LORD with his hard and
great and strong sword will punish Levi'athan
the fleeing serpent, Levi'athan the twisting
serpent, and he will slay the dragon that is in
the sea.
2 In that day:
"A pleasant vineyard, sing of it!
3   I, the LORD, am its keeper;

every moment I water it.
Lest any one harm it,
   I guard it night and day;
4   I have no wrath.
Would that I had thorns and briers to battle!
   I would set out against them,
   I would burn them up together.
5 Or let them lay hold of my protection,
   let them make peace with me,
   let them make peace with me."
6 In days to come[a] Jacob shall take root,
   Israel shall blossom and put forth shoots,
   and fill the whole world with fruit.
7 Has he smitten them as he smote those who smote them?
   Or have they been slain as their slayers were slain?
8 Measure by measure,[b] by exile thou didst contend with them;

Psalm 110:1 (RSV)
Assurance of Victory for God's Priest-King
A Psalm of David.
110 The LORD says to my lord:
"Sit at my right hand,
till I make your enemies your footstool."
2 The LORD sends forth from Zion
   your mighty scepter.
   Rule in the midst of your foes!
3 Your people will offer themselves freely

on the day you lead your host
   upon the holy mountains.[a]
From the womb of the morning
   like dew your youth[b] will come to you.
4 The LORD has sworn
   and will not change his mind,
"You are a priest for ever
   after the order of Melchiz'edek."
5 The Lord is at your right hand;
   he will shatter kings on the day of his wrath.
6 He will execute judgment among the
nations,
   filling them with corpses;
he will shatter chiefs[c]
   over the wide earth.
7 He will drink from the brook by the way;
   therefore he will lift up his head.

OUR RESURRECTION

Our Resurrection is illustrated in the below Old Testament passages. The Resurrection is not the product of imagination; rather, it is made possible through our love for God and Jesus.

Ezekiel 37:1 (RSV)
The Valley of Dry Bones
37 The hand of the LORD was upon me, and he brought me out by the Spirit of the LORD,

and set me down in the midst of the valley;[a] it was full of bones.2 And he led me round among them; and behold, there were very many upon the valley;[b] and lo, they were very dry. 3 And he said to me, "Son of man, can these bones live?" And I answered, "O Lord GOD, thou knowest." 4 Again he said to me, "Prophesy to these bones, and say to them, O dry bones, hear the word of the LORD. 5 Thus says the Lord GOD to these bones: Behold, I will cause breath[c] to enter you, and you shall live. 6 And I will lay sinews upon you, and will cause flesh to come upon you, and cover you with skin, and put breath[d] in you, and you shall live; and you shall know that I am the LORD." 7 So I prophesied as I was commanded; and as I prophesied, there was a noise, and behold, a rattling; and the bones came together, bone to its bone. 8 And as I looked, there were sinews on them, and flesh had come upon them, and skin had covered them; but there was no breath in them. 9 Then he said to me, "Prophesy to the breath, prophesy, son of man, and say to the breath,[e] Thus says the Lord GOD: Come from the four winds, O breath,[f] and breathe upon these slain, that they may live." 10 So I prophesied as he commanded me, and the breath came into them, and they lived, and stood upon their feet, an exceedingly great host. 11 Then he said to me, "Son of man, these bones are the whole house of Israel. Behold, they say, 'Our bones are dried up, and our hope is lost; we are clean cut off.' 12 Therefore prophesy, and say to them, Thus says the Lord GOD: Behold, I will open your graves, and raise you from your graves, O my people; and I will bring you home into the land of Israel. 13 And you shall know that I am the LORD, when I open your graves, and raise you from your graves, O my people. 14 And I will put my Spirit within you, and you shall live, and I will place you in your own land; then you shall know that I, the LORD, have spoken, and I have done it, says the LORD."

Hosea 13:14 (RSV)
14 Shall I ransom them from the power of Sheol?
   Shall I redeem them from Death?
O Death, where[a] are your plagues?
   O Sheol, where[b] is your destruction?
   Compassion is hid from my eyes.

Here, our Lord taunts Death revealing His will for our Resurrection.

Isaiah 26:19 (RSV)
Judah's Song of Victory

19 Thy dead shall live, their bodies[c] shall rise.

O dwellers in the dust, awake and sing for joy!
For thy dew is a dew of light,
   and on the land of the shades thou wilt let it fall.

Daniel 12:1 (RSV)
The Resurrection of the Dead
12 "At that time shall arise Michael, the great prince who has charge of your people. And there shall be a time of trouble, such as never has been since there was a nation till that time; but at that time your people shall be delivered, every one whose name shall be found written in the book. 2 And many of those who sleep in the dust of the earth shall awake, some to everlasting life, and some to shame and everlasting contempt. 3 And those who are wise shall shine like the brightness of the firmament; and those who turn many to righteousness, like the stars for ever and ever. 4 But you, Daniel, shut up the words, and seal the book, until the time of the end. Many shall run to and fro, and knowledge shall increase."

IN THE SPIRIT OF TRUTH:
IDENTIFYING MY THREE THEOLOGICAL
TREATISES IN CHURCH TRADITION

JAMES THOMAS ANGELIDIS

I see myself in Jesus Christ's words when he said, "every scribe who has been trained for the kingdom of heaven is like a householder who brings out of his treasure what is new and what is old" (Matthew 13:52). The Lord's cited saying is not a riddle to be wrestled with or parable to be pondered; rather, it is a metaphor that reveals a truth about theological treasures, a metaphor that elucidates, a metaphor that is as clear as water ready for drinking.

I cherish the Church Fathers and Patristic literature and not only learned theology from them but have imitated their writing style and goals with

my three theological treatises in the positive
apologetics manner. Apologetics writing is a defense:

> Typically these consisted of what are
> called negative apologetics, wherein a writer
> takes up a series of challenges to Christian
> belief, and shows them to lack the power that
> their proponents think they have.
> We also sometimes see positive
> apologetics, an argument that attempts to
> provide its audience with some fresh positive
> reasons for belief, intended to convince others
> who are not yet convinced of the truth of the
> Christian faith (Mathewes, *The Great
> Courses, The City of God, Guidebook*, 87).

My book - *In the Name of Salvation: Three
Theological Treatises* - is a positive apologetics work.
Saint Augustine of Hippo is my dearest friend
and his *The City of God* is the second most important
book I have ever read - preceded only by the Holy
Bible. Augustine showed us with his words the
earthly City of Man and the heavenly City of God like
no one else before. It was not dictated to him by
anyone before him. His work is unprecedented. He
observed it, dug deep into Scripture and revealed to
us eternal latent truths. Like no one before, he
illuminated to everyone after him the nature of the
cosmos with his Scriptural insights. Truly, he
brought out of his treasure what is new and what is

old. I have carried on that tradition with my three theological treatises.

Church Fathers, like Augustine, saw truths in ancient Greek philosophy, particularly that of Plato. I see truths in Taoist and Hindu philosophy/theology. After my first university degree, at age 22, I immersed myself in the six great world religions' scriptures. I wrote about this intense two-year period in my book *Writings* in my article "A Theological Memoir." From this period, I began to see Christian truths in Taoist and Hindu philosophy/theology. Henry David Thoreau - one of America's best - wrote, "That age will be rich indeed when those relics which we call Classics, and the still older and more than classic but even less known Scriptures of the nations, shall have still further accumulated, when the Vaticans shall be filled with Vedas and Zendavestas and Bibles, with Homers and Dantes and Shakespeares, and all the centuries to come shall have successively deposited their trophies in the forum of the world. By such a pile we may hope to scale heaven at last (Thoreau, *Walden, Reading*). I - James Thomas Angelidis - am the product and fruit of this now realized prophesied era. Like never before, today, an individual can study the world religions' scriptures and witness common truths among them. All that is needed are discipline and desire.

In the 20th century, the Catholic Church spoke about a theology called "Hierarchy of Truths" to initiate Christian ecumenism and interfaith dialogue.

The Hierarchy of Truths Theology is very real and applicable to Christianity, religion, philosophy and humanity. God - the Great Sower - planted seeds across the world, seeds that took root and grew in the world's religions. Truths can be found in them all; however, what is said about the Jews is true - they were the Chosen People, they were God's Vineyard (Isaiah 5:1-7). For from them grew the True Vine - God's Son Jesus the Christ (Psalm 80:8-19) (John 15:1-17). I am just trying to be one of our Lord's branches and bear fruit for him because I love him so much. I believe my work can help serve God and the world in the economy of Salvation.

God, Jesus and Christian theology are eternal, limitless and unbound. They are so big that much can escape articulation until brought to attention. We see this in "Homoousios" and "Theotokos" theology which developed and blossomed after Jesus. They were unprecedented formulations, but are theologically appropriate. In this way, the theology in my treatises is similar.

The most traditional, parochial and conservative Saint Vincent of Lerins taught us in his *Commonitorium* that "theologians should say things newly without saying new things" (Guarino, *Vincent of Lerins*, 86). My work is a new presentation of traditional theology. There is no new theology in my treatises; rather, an affirmation of old theology presented in a new way (said newly). The deposit is guarded.

- The "Supreme Transformation" theology is based on Saint Melito of Sardis's "analogy" or "preliminary sketch" theology - his prefiguring theology - as it appears in his *On Pascha*.

- The "Agape into Eternity" theology is based on the Trisagion Prayers theology that many Orthodox Christians, like me, pray every morning and every night.

- The "Messiah Jesus" theology is based on Jewish prophetic theology as it appears in the Old Testament.

I spell this out to reassure readers that the theology in my work is not fabricated or an invention and that it is, in fact, within the tradition of the One Holy Catholic and Apostolic Church.

There is nothing new about God or Jesus's natures or the means to Salvation in my three theological treatises. They are observations that are authentic, honest, insightful and true. They illuminate, enlighten, elucidate, unfold, uncover, unearth, disclose, reveal. They are the result of the Holy Spirit's Agape in me. I was compelled to write out of agape for God and neighbor. They are authentic scholarly Scriptural insights. They are progressive explanatory clarifications and are supplementations that add further fullness to Christian theology. *In the Name of Salvation* is meant to save people and unite people with Almighty God by means of traditional theology in a fresh way.

My three theological treatises are not lies, not transgressions, not trespassings, not fabrications, not inventions, not novelties, not adulterations, not corruptions, not distortions, not perversions.

My book *In the Name of Salvation* is a part of the prophecy told to Daniel: "those who are wise shall shine like the brightness of the firmament; and those who turn many to righteousness, like the stars for ever and ever. 4 But you, Daniel, shut up the words, and seal the book, until the time of the end. Many shall run to and fro, and knowledge shall increase" (Daniel 12:3-4). Yes, indeed, knowledge shall increase.

So, I conclude and tell you to not turn away from my works because of the hardness of your hearts. And, do not fear. Open your hearts with the Spirit of Truth. Allow the Spirit of Truth to guide you and you will see truth in my works.

WORKS CITED
(in order referenced)

THE SUPREME TRANSFORMATION - WATER
INTO WINE

- *Bible*, Revised Standard Version (RSV).
- Lao Tzu. *Tao Te Ching: The Definitive Edition* (trans. by Jonathan Star). New York: Tarcher/Putnam, 2001.
- Lao-Tzu. *Tao Te Ching* (trans. by Stephen Addiss and Stanley Lombardo). Indianapolis: Hackett Publishing Company, 1993.
- Lao Tsu. *Tao Te Ching* (trans. by Gia-Fu Feng and Jane English). New York: Vintage Books, 1989.
- Lao Tzu. *Tao Teh Ching* (trans. by John C.H. Wu). Boston: Shambhala Publications, 1990.
- *World Book Encyclopedia 1966*, "Wine." Chicago: Field Enterprises Educational Corporation, 1965.
- Melito of Sardis. *On Pascha* (trans. by Alistair Stewart-Sykes). Crestwood: St Vladimir's Seminary Press, 2001.

- Toussaint, Stanley D. "The Significance of the First Sign in John's Gospel." *Bibliotheca Sacra*, Jan-Mar 1977: 49-51.

AGAPE INTO ETERNITY
- *Bible*, Revised Standard Version (RSV).
- *Upanishads* (trans. Swami Prabhavananda and Frederick Manchester). New York: Signet Classic, 2002.
- *Bhagavad-Gita* (trans. Swami Prabhavananda and Christopher Isherwood). New York: Signet Classic, 2002.
- Antiochian Orthodox Christian Archdiocese of North America. *A Pocket Prayer Book for Orthodox Christians*. Englewood: Antiochian Orthodox Christian Archdiocese, 1956.
- Kreeft, Peter. *The God Who Loves You*. San Francisco: Ignatius Press, 2004.
- *Nicene Creed*. Greek Orthodox Archdiocese of America.

THE MESSIAH JESUS
- *Bible*, Revised Standard Version (RSV).
- Jennings, Peter. *ABC News Presents The Search for Jesus [DVD]*. ABC News Productions, 2000.

Not cited - though a bibliographical reference:
- Briggs, Charles Augustus. *Messianic Prophecy*. New York: Charles Scribner's Sons, 1886.

IN THE SPIRIT OF TRUTH
- *Bible*, Revised Standard Version (RSV).
- Mathewes, Charles. "Books That Matter: The City of God." *The Great Courses* DVD Course with Guidebook. Chantilly: The Teaching Company, 2016.
- Augustine [Saint]. *The City of God* (ed. and trans. by Marcus Dods). New York: The Modern Library, 1993.
- Angelidis, James Thomas. *Writings*. www.jtangelidis.com: James Thomas Angelidis, 2016; 2017.
- Thoreau, Henry David. *Walden*. New York: Signet Classic, 1942.
- Guarino, Thomas G. *Vincent of Lérins and the Development of Christian Doctrine.* Grand Rapids: Baker Academic, 2013.

www.ingramcontent.com/pod-product-compliance
Lightning Source LLC
Chambersburg PA
CBHW072020040426

42447CB00009B/1674